Dear Reverend Alewine,
 This book is due in part to the faithful work you did in my life and in the life of Joe Stasiukaitis. Only God knows the far

God's Little Bird
A War Orphan's Story

reach of your influence on the lives of thousands of us.

By

Laura McCurry Knotts

This book is just one example. Happy New Year! I love you!
Laura

Preface

About 75 years ago, in 1944, hundreds of thousands of Baltic citizens were caught in the bloody crossfire of the Soviets and Nazis and forced to flee their homelands.

Lithuanian citizens had suffered brutal persecution for years during earlier Soviet and German occupations, and by the end of World War II, only 1 million Lithuanians remained out of a population of 3 million.

Similarly, in what became known as the Lithuanian Diaspora, only one in three of those who fled Lithuania survived. These 60,000 surviving refugees were detained and sheltered in German Displaced Persons (DP) Camps. They called themselves "Dievo Pauksteliai" or "God's Little Birds."

This is the remarkable story of one such refugee, a young boy named Jouzas, who was wrenched from everything he knew and everyone he held dear on a cold October day in 1944 and forced to fly for his life, leaving his mother, brothers, and sisters behind.

However, like the story of Joseph in the Bible who was forced into exile far from his homeland and family, God had His hand on this little Lithuanian boy.

in His providential grace, God brought Joseph safely through a journey of exile, loss, persecution, and despair into a new life in America where Joe's story was transformed into one of belonging, restoration, hope, and purpose.

Part One:
Child of Lithuania

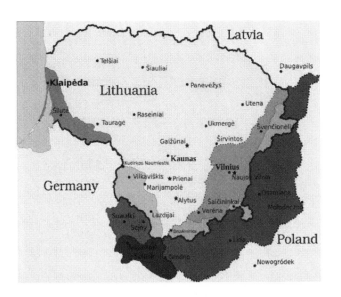

Chapter 1

God Will Add

"The Lord was with Joseph." (Genesis 39:2) "You intended to harm me, but God intended it for good to accomplish what is now being done, the saving of many lives." (Genesis 50:20)

Their house was like many of the other homes in Naujininkai, a small village in the Vilkaviskis district of Lithuania.

Grandfather Stasiukaitis had labored to build it, wrestling the large boulders strewn across the countryside into place to form a foundation which he then filled with rocks and mud and covered with clay to make the floor.

He had built the walls two feet thick to keep out the winter cold ward off the heat in summer. The fireplace was the main feature of the u-shaped house, and it took up an entire wall. A small pot-bellied stove much like a kiln sat in a corner of the fireplace.

The chimney flue line traveled all the length of the room on the ground like a stone bench to carry away the smoke and heat the entire room. Grandfather completed the home by roofing it with thatch and cutting in two windows.

The long winters began in October with numbing cold and house-covering snow which did not thaw until late April or early May.

Once the snow came, it froze and stayed, adding layer upon layer all through the winter, so that they had to dig a connecting tunnel from the house to the barn and stable to care for the animals.

If the winter's arrival was cold and sudden, it could take two days to dig a tunnel to get to the cattle to feed them. Sometimes the snow drifts covered the house, and they would have to sled off the roof when they wanted to leave the house.

Their father, Tomas, grew up in the sturdy house his father built. When he was old enough, he worked alongside his father on the farm every day except for Sunday when the whole family would make the walk to the neighboring village of Pajevonys to its Cathedral to worship.

Tomas was never one to shirk the hard labor of farming, and he was tired of living under Russian rule which banned the Lithuanian language and suppressed the Catholic religion.

When recruiters from Britain came and promised Lithuanian farm workers that a bright future awaited them in the English mines, Tomas bid his parents farewell and left the farm to seek his fortune in England.

But life wasn't any easier, and as events led to the beginning of the First World War, it became even harder to live in English communities among people who became mistrustful and suspicious of him, often mistaking him for a hated Russian.

Then one day a letter waited for him when he came in after a long day of work in the mines. It was from his parents. His mother wrote that they were getting old, and it was becoming too hard to keep up with the farm work.

She pleaded with Tomas to come home and live with them on the small farm and take it over. Tomas sat and thought about the letter. He admitted to himself that he was unhappy in England.

He wasn't getting ahead, and he didn't fit in. He was tired of the suspicion and hostility, and he missed his home and family. He packed up his few belongings and left to make the long trip back home.

Tomas settled in back at home. He married a local girl, Ona, and within a few years they had a daughter and a son. He worked hard to wring enough living from the small farm to care for his young family and also support his aging parents.

In order to own the whole farm, Tomas had to pay off his brother and two sisters and even divide the milk of their one cow between his family and parents, but he was young and strong, and conditions were better after the war.

He just barely managed to make the payments and still have enough left to provide for Ona, eight-year-old Terese, and five year old Jonas. And they had another child on the way.

Then disaster struck. In May 1926, Ona died giving birth to Salomi, and at 37 years old, Tomas was left alone to care for two grieving children and a needy newborn.

He nearly despaired as he thought of raising his children alone while trying to support them and his aging parents with whatever he could get from three acres, one cow, a horse, two sheep, and some pigs.

However, Tomas was a man of great faith and had always faithfully attended mass. So even when his grief was fresh, he made the five kilometer walk to the Cathedral.

As he walked, he prayed, and he asked God to help him find a way to care for his children and his parents. When he entered the cathedral for worship that morning, he was at peace, knowing that God heard his prayer.

Then he saw Magdelena, and he knew God had answered. Three months later, they were married.

Tomas thanked God for providing him with a wife and a mother for Terese, Jonas, and baby Salomi. A thirty-year-old spinster, Magdelena was grateful that God had heard her prayers and provided her with a good husband and a home.

Tomas was known throughout his community as a good, kind man and as very hard worker who was always ready to help his neighbors. He didn't drink; he lived for his family, and he never missed mass.

Like Tomas, Magdelena was well-loved and known to be a tireless worker and a woman of great faith. As the years went on, Magdelena accepted that fact that she could not bear children, but she loved Tomas's children and was the only mother Salomi had ever known.

The children loved her, too, and life settled into a happy rhythm of work, worship, friends, and family. Then in 1931, after nearly five years of marriage, Magdelena was surprised to realize that God had answered her prayers again.

That year, she and Tomas were overjoyed by the birth of Vitas, followed in 1932 by the birth of Antonus. In 1934, they had yet another son, and they named him Jouzas, which means "God will add."

In 1935, when Magdelena was nearly forty, a baby girl, little Anele, was born. It was a complete and happy home for the family of nine, full of love and faith and laughter.

Tomas and Magdelena enjoyed sharing the household chores, cooking and caring for their growing family and managing the small farm together, tending to the animals and the garden.

Magdelena and tiny Anele slept in the same bed, a wooden box with straw and a sheet, and two-year-old Jouzas laughed in the morning to see them wake up with straw sticking out of their hair and clothes.

As Jouzas grew, he loved following Tomas around when he was taking care of the animals. Little Anele made them all laugh, and he and Vitas and Antonus always found time away from chores to make up games and run and shout and wrestle together.

For a faithful Catholic family, Sunday was the most important day of the week. Papa never missed going to the Cathedral in Pajevonys.

Jouzas eagerly looked forward to every other Sunday, when it was his turn to go with Papa and wear the carefully kept church clothes Antonus had worn the week before on his turn.

Jouzas anticipated the special day all week, and Mama didn't have to remind him to wash up the night before or tell him twice that it was time to go to bed.

He hurried into bed. The sooner he went to sleep on Saturday night, the sooner the morning would come when he could go with Papa to thank God in His grand house.

Jouzas woke as soon as the darkness began to turn from black to gray and waited for Papa to say it was time to get up and put on the special church clothes that Mama had laid out for him to wear.

He quickly washed his face and hands and solemnly dressed and ate the breakfast Mama had prepared for him. When Papa said it was time, he picked up the clogs and carried them.

He hurried to keep up with his brothers and sister as they walked through the hills. When they reached the holy ground of the Cathedral, they stopped and put their clogs on over their cold bare feet before joining the other worshippers inside.

The huge brick and stone structure with its high graceful arches filled Jouzas with awe. Jouzas was proud to file in with the rest of his family and sit beside his father in peaceful reverence. After mass, they all removed their clogs and carried them home.

When it turned cold, Jouzas was thankful to find woolen boots, laid out beside the Sunday clothes, that Mama had made to keep his feet from freezing during the long, cold walk to church.

When the snow piled up so high that it was over their heads, his big brother Jonas took him and Antonus and Vitas sledding off of the roof. One time the sled flew through the snow so fast that they couldn't stop it, and it headed straight to the pond.

They tumbled off just before it reached the pond's icy edge, but as they picked themselves up, they helplessly watched it slide out onto the thin ice. The ice cracked, and their sled plunged under the water not to be seen again until the spring.

Farm home in Vilkaviskis

Cathedral in Pajevonys

Chapter 2

Fatherless

"Blessed are you who are poor, for yours is the kingdom of God. Blessed are you who hunger now, for you will be satisfied. Blessed are you who weep now, for you will laugh." (Luke 6: 20-21)

In this simple, happy home, as the youngest of four lively brothers and two loving older sisters, Jouzas enjoyed a carefree, fun-filled childhood. Then, on a cold day in March, when Jouzas was five, everything changed.

Jouzas heard Jonas calling for him. He ran to his older brother, and Jonas just took him by the hand and led him into the house. He stopped just inside the door.

Jouzas stood there as his eyes adjusted to the dark. He was confused by the jumble of hushed conversation, and he grew uneasy when he heard the sounds of people crying and someone moaning.

"Poor Tomas," someone said. "What will Magdelena do now?" he heard another ask. "Seven children, how will she manage on her own?"

Where was his mama? He couldn't see more than the clay floor at his feet and a forest of legs surrounding him, hiding his mother from him. He thought she might be by the stove by the fireplace, but he couldn't see her.

He cried out, "Mama! Mama, where are you?" A hand on his shoulder gently moved him forward, and the sea of legs turned toward him and parted to form a path that led to the bed where his father had lain for the last few days with a headache.

Then he saw him, his Papa, still and white as the snow outside. Jouzas began to tremble, and his chest grew tight in fear. His mother sat in the chair by the bed with her face in her hands, and he heard a sound he had never heard before. She was crying.

Jouzas turned and fled past the hands that reached out for him. He found the door and rushed back into the cold where his breath came out hard and fast, and his sobbing turned into little white clouds.

Slipping on the snow, he ran into the tunnel under the snow drift and crawled into the stable. He stayed and listened to the cow breathe and the low chuckling of the ducks and the snuffling of the pig until he cried himself asleep.

After the funeral, Magdelena had little time to grieve. She gathered the weeping children around her, Anele, Antonus, Vitas, and Jouzas. The older ones, Salomi, Jonas, and Terese, stood silently beside her with reddened, anxious eyes.

She said their Papa had a tumor in his brain that burst, and he had gone to heaven. She needed them to help her pray and work hard and find a way to keep all of them together and food on the table.

Soon Magdelena, now in her forties, would discover that another mouth to feed would be joining the family. In December, she gave birth to Bernardos, a son who would never see his father, Tomas's eighth and youngest child.

The funeral of Tomas Stasiukaitis, 1940

Chapter 3

The End of Childhood

*"For I know the plans I have for you, declares
the Lord, plans for welfare and not for evil, to
give you a future and a hope." (Jeremiah 29:11)*

After Papa died, Jouzas was always
hungry. He would dream of meat and
enough clothes and a big stove that would
keep them all warm.

Jouzas never ate meat except on a
holiday. It was always cabbage, potatoes,
carrots, beets, peas, or beans. They
butchered one pig in the fall, and they had to
make it last all year.

When Mama could get a salt herring,
they would feast on the flesh one day, and
then they would carefully save the head and
bones, so Mama could make soup the
following day.

She would add water, a little pepper,
and maybe some potatoes to make the
soup, and sometimes, they had bread and
sour milk to go with it.

Only at Christmas time, Mama would make sure they had some kind of meat. Christmas dinner would be sauerkraut, potatoes, and a little meat, the rare treat.

Christmas was the only time the whole family would get together. All of Magdalena's children lived with her in the small house, except for Jonas and Teresa, who were grown and away working all year, and only able to come home at Christmas.

It was a hard time. Magdelena not only worked hard on the farm, she took on jobs knitting gloves and socks and spinning yarn. She made butter that the children took around and sold along with the eggs to have enough money for necessities.

Their neighbors did what they could to help the struggling family. One neighbor made them wooden shoes. Jonas Raila and his wife didn't have any children of their own, and they always welcomed the children.

They frequently turned up at the Raila's house at mealtimes because kind Mrs. Raila never failed to have something for the hungry children to eat.

But life didn't get any better. It got worse. Jouzas felt sad for his mother. She was a wonderful woman, and she worked long into the night, doing the best she could.

Jouzas watched her as she worked and saw her lips constantly move in prayer. Despite her prayers, the day came when there was not enough food for everyone to eat.

It wasn't her fault; she did everything she could after Papa died, but she could no longer support the family. The time had come to send more of the children to work if they were to live.

Terese had gotten a job working as a maid for the Paukstys family. One day in early April, Farmer Paukstys came to the house and told Mama that he needed a boy to tend the cows, and he agreed to hire eight-year-old Antonus.

Then he looked over at Jouzas and began to talk to Mama about taking another boy with him to be their "Hawk Fighter" from April until October. The hawk fighter would herd the ducks and keep the hawks away.

This was an important job because the Paukstys used the ducks for feathers, eggs, and meat. They would pay the little hired boy a small amount, but more importantly, Mama knew that this meant the child would eat.

Jouzas, who had turned six, had been able to go to school for the past few months, but he wouldn't be going to school anymore; he was old enough to go to work, and he, too, left with Mr. Paukstys to be his hawk fighter.

Antonus was proud and excited at first to be a cow herder, but eventually he got tired of watching cows. One day, he took them out and left them. He didn't want to tell his mother, so he slept in the barn that night so she wouldn't know.

Mrs. Paukstys, angry that Antonus left the cows untended, came and complained to Magdelena and told her that because Antonus had abandoned his responsibility, he had lost his chance to help his family.

However, the younger Jouzas faced his new life with determination. He worked hard to help Mama. He would not quit and have Mama think he was lazy or irresponsible like his big brothers Jonas and Antonus.

Day after day, he took good care of the ducks from sunup to sundown. Jouzas wasn't hungry now. The Paukstys fed him.

He had clothes too, but he didn't like them. They hurt his skin. He had raw places on his arms and legs where the rough cloth rubbed.

His feet hurt too. They bled every night after he ran barefoot in the field over sharp stones and dry stalks chasing hawks all day.

At night, he would think of Mama and wonder what Vitas and Antonus were doing. How were Anele and baby Bernadas? He hoped they had plenty to eat. But at least his mother didn't have to worry about feeding him until he came home in October.

Jouzas waited eagerly for the winter to come when he would be home with everyone again. When the cold weather came, Mrs. Paukstys took Jouzas home, and he watched her as she measured out his pay and gave it to Mama: ten pounds of wheat!

Mama looked at Jouzas and smiled. After Mrs. Paukstys left, she hugged him close and said, "Jouzas, your hard work will help all of us eat this winter."

The next year, Jouzas watched the Paukstys' cows. He stood for hours in the fields tending them. In the cold weather, when his bare feet felt like painful blocks of ice, Jouzas looked for fresh steaming piles of cow dung to stand in to thaw them out.

That year, Mr. Paukstys sometimes drank too much and got violent. Jouzas was miserable. He couldn't stand it anymore, so he left and went home to his mother and begged her not to make him go back.

After a few moments of silence, she looked at him with tear-filled eyes and responded sorrowfully, "My dear child, we don't have a choice."

Somehow, she found the words that convinced Jouzas that he must go back. Years later, Jouzas would remember this and think about how hard it must have been for her to say those words to her beloved child.

The family of Tomas and Magdelena
Stasiukaitis

28

Chapter 4

Occupation

"Woe to those who make unjust laws, to those who issue oppressive decrees, to deprive the poor of their rights and withhold justice from the oppressed of my people, making widows their prey and robbing the fatherless. What will you do on the day of reckoning, when disaster comes from afar? To whom will you run for help? Where will you leave your riches?" (Isaiah 10:1-3)

After WWI, Lithuania enjoyed years of independence, but the Russians took over Lithuania again on June 14, 1940, and from the beginning, the occupation was terrible.

First, the Soviets took over all the land, and no one owned their own land anymore. A Lithuanian had to get permission even if he wanted to go to see a neighbor or just needed to go through someone's farm to get somewhere.

Persecution increased against all Lithuanians, particularly the Catholics. They enforced old laws forbidding Lithuanians to speak Lithuanian in public and forced them to speak Russian only.

To make matters worse, their own Lithuanian government was corrupt and complicit in the murder and deportation of its own people. Lithuanians were faced with fighting their own government and being forced to work with the Russians.

Then even more terrible persecution began. Educated and religious people in their community began to disappear, and no one had any idea what had happened to them. Next, anyone who had anything to do with the government disappeared too.

Neighbors vanished in the night. Word came back that the communists had shipped people off to work camps. Some were sent to Siberia, and others were simply killed. Those who were left lived in fear and hunger. Food was scarce and getting scarcer.

During this time, Jouzas left the Paukstys and went to work for the Rudzevicius family as a shepherd. The Rudzevicius' farm was much farther away from his house, and now he was only able to go home on Sundays.

The Germans invaded a year later on June 22, 1941. It was a Sunday morning, and Jouzas was taking cows out as he usually did before going home by noon for his half day off.

He planned to start early to have more time with his family. The farm was on a hill with a little brook running by, and a main highway of gravel ran from Germany to Russia right by the farm.

At 10:00 am, he heard planes, and when he looked up, he saw them flying around overhead. An hour later, he heard the army marching down the main road that came past the farm.

As they came into view, he was astonished that the soldiers were so uniform, the same height and all blonde, and great numbers of them kept marching and marching past.

Jouzas couldn't get his cows across the road. A leader of the thousands of soldiers in rows that were 12 men wide stopped the march to let little eight-year-old Jouzas go across with the cows. He took them into the barn and headed back to the house.

The starving Lithuanians poured out into the streets to welcome the Germans. All of the village of Vilkaviskis celebrated the departure of the Russians.

The Russian army was so poor that even the captured Russians, who the Germans put to work on the farm as prison-laborers where Jouzas worked, seemed relieved that the conquering Germans might come with the hope of food.

Lithuania was under German occupation. And they hadn't fired a shot. The people's relief and celebration were short-lived. By July, the Germans had taken over all the Baltic countries, and they began a persecution that extended to all people.

During the German occupation, the German army required everyone to register all their livestock, every chicken, pig, and cow. Officers inspected all the Lithuanians homes and property to make sure all Lithuanians had complied and requisitioned livestock for "payment."

But Jonas refused to register their pig. The villagers helped each other get around the Germans. When the post office received notice of an upcoming inspection, word passed from neighbor to neighbor: "The German army is coming to inspect!"

With each inspection, Jonas managed to quickly move the pig to the other side of the hill and hide it, and time after time, the Germans never suspected the ruse. Finally, one Sunday in November, Jonas finally decided it was time to kill the pig.

Normally a farmer would kill a farm animal with a single shot to the skull, but they didn't dare risk firing a shot and having the Germans swarm them.

They decided the best way to kill it quietly was to smash it on the head with a hammer. The children chased it out of the barn, and Jonas caught it with the heavy hammer in hand.

He swung the hammer high and gave it a mighty blow on the head. To their horror, instead of dropping down dead or least falling senseless to the ground, the huge hog indignantly sat back on its butt and started to pierce the air with its squeals.

As the squeals continued and gained in volume, Magdelena panicked, declared she wasn't going to have any part of it, hooked up the wagon. and raced away from them.

They eventually managed to kill the hog, and every bite of meat was a satisfying reminder of their small victory in their resistance against the Germans.

Jouzas and his family continued to live through the German occupation with the knowledge that every day German soldiers rounded people up and shot them.

By December, people throughout the surrounding Vilkaviskis district realized that thousands of Vilkaviskis Jews, an integral, respected, and large part of their community, were disappearing, and no one had any idea where they had gone.

Years later, the remaining citizens would discover that every single Jew had been slaughtered, and most of them had been killed in one horrifying, murderous day.

Maybe at times Jonas could be a problem for his mother, but Jouzas was proud of him for joining the guerillas and glad that he had a brother who was brave enough to fight the hated German army.

Soviet Invasion
1940

German Occupation 1941

Part Two:
Stranger in a Strange Land

38

Chapter 5

Exodus

"Be strong and courageous. Do not be afraid or terrified because of them, for the LORD your God goes with you; He will never leave you nor forsake you." (Deuteronomy 31:6)

In the summer of 1944, the Russians advanced on Lithuania again. At this time, Jouzas was living with Mr. and Mrs. Ruzvycius and working for the "old man" as a shepherd, watching his cows and sheep.

When the Germans took control from Russia in 1941, they put Russian prisoners to work on the farms, and Jouzas learned some Russian from prisoners who were working on the Ruzvycius farm.

That summer he heard rumors that the Russians were steadily advancing on the Germans. He saw the Germans digging foxholes and planting landmines throughout the fields all around a long hill that was in the middle of the farmer's fields.

A church surrounded by trees stood on top of the hill and was visible for miles away. The Germans stretched out barbed wire in the fields all around the church, and then they blew up its steeple so that the Russians couldn't use it for navigation.

The Germans commandeered the Ruzvycius's house as their headquarters and forced the family out. They moved to their place closer to the German border and further away from the Germans and their landmines and barbed wire.

Jonas, now 24, spent the past three years making trouble for the invading Germans. Now that the Russians were vanquishing the Germans to reoccupy Lithuania, he used his experienced tactics in resistance to cause trouble for them, too.

However, the Russians discovered his identify, set a trap, and captured him. Jouzas felt sick when he learned that the Russians had sentenced Jonas to three years of slave labor in a Siberian labor camp.

Jouzas had already lived through the horror of people disappearing under the German occupation, and he knew that they did not return from labor camps. It might as well have been a death sentence.

When they took Jonas away and put him on the prison train to Siberia, Jouzas, Magdelena, and his brothers and sisters grieved, doubting that they would ever see their prankster, daredevil, fiercely patriotic oldest brother again.

Then on a fall day in 1944, a day Jouzas would never forget, Antonas came to the farm. He found Jouzas in the fields watching the sheep and cows. Antonas urged Jouzas,

> "Hurry and get your things, Jouzas, You've got to come home. Mother is afraid of what is going to happen when the Russians get here, and she wants us to be together."

Jouzas wanted to leave right away, but he knew the elderly couple in their seventies needed his help to prepare for the coming turmoil and upheaval.

> "Antonas," he said, shaking his head, "I can't come yet. I have to do what I can for old man Ruzvycius and his wife,

first. Tell Mama that I'll come home on Sunday."

However, that night, after Antonas returned home without him, the Soviets started their fierce bombing campaign, and Jouzas would not be able to keep his promise.

The following morning, when Jouzas took out the cattle, it was beautiful and sunny, but when he rounded the corner and looked to the east, he saw that the sky was black with flak from Russian bombs and dirt from exploding mine fields.

As he watched in stunned amazement, the blackness swallowed the sun. The air smelled of dust and burning, and the cattle took off running in all directions.

Jouzas tried to catch them and bring them back under control, but finally, he gave up trying and ran to the farmer's house.

The Soviets relentlessly bombed all the surrounding area throughout the long day. Word spread that everyone was leaving the village and retreating to the safety of Germany.

The Ruzvyciuses were terrified of the Russians, so they decided to abandon the farm and flee to Germany the next morning. They urged Jouzas to come with them and assured him that his family would be joining the mass retreat.

They hurriedly gathered up their belongings and packed everything into two wagons to be pulled by their four horses.

While they were packing, they discovered an unexploded bomb lodged in the attic. That night, the entire household moved into the attached barn in hopes that its two-foot-thick walls would provide them with better protection.

The roar of Russian bombing awoke them the next morning and continued without ceasing throughout the day. They were frantic to move out, but it was impossible to reach the road.

They huddled together in the cellar for protection and waited out the interminable day. When they finally crept out of the cellar, they stared around them in shock.

A large black hole gaped in the ground where the neighbor's house had been. Nothing remained of the house or their neighbors, only the stark evidence of a direct hit.

The Ruzvycius's horses and one of their loaded wagons were gone, too. Nothing could be done except to repack what they could into the remaining wagon. They fled at dawn.

The terrified group hurried to reach the highway and join their wagon to the exodus of Lithuanian families. The German army, in full retreat, was also on the highway pulling their artillery with them.

The Russians started bombing the highway. The bombing became such a constant, numbing presence that Jouzas felt like he was playing a nightmarish game.

The rule was to run as the bombs fell through the air, and the object was to find a ditch and lay down in it just before they hit the ground.

First, he became aware of the distant drone of planes; then he watched the sky turn dark like an oncoming storm. This was the signal to find the nearest ditch and dive in, not giving a thought to whatever might be in the ditch with him.

After the roar of their propellers faded away, he crawled out wet and covered with mud, but alive to do it all over again. Jouzas forgot to be afraid as he automatically moved into action, wearily stumbling through the exhausting game.

To Jouzas' relief, they left the highway and went into the country. For two weeks they stayed off the main road and slowly made their way toward the German border.

As they crossed the border out of Lithuania and moved deeper into Germany, they passed the abandoned farms of families who also had precipitately fled the oncoming disaster.

Jouzas observed the evidence of their frantic upheaval. Cows bawled to be milked, and Jouzas often found warm, uneaten meals on their kitchen tables. At the first town they came to, he found a bloody watch left at the drinking well. The old man took it.

Jouzas' world was in total chaos. He longed for his family and constantly searched the steady stream of refugees for a sign of them.

He told himself that they had escaped into Germany, too, and he wondered if they had stayed on the road, or if they, like him, had left the road for the safety of the countryside.

But at night, when he remembered the downpour of bombs and the fields surrounding their home so thickly sown with exploding mines, he had to fight off the hopeless certainty that they couldn't possibly have escaped, and must all be dead.

In the weeks that followed, the Germans marshalled the refugees into one place, Koenigsberg. There they separated the refugees into those who could work and those who were too old or too young to be useful.

They took any horses and wagons and marched the old people and children away into open boxcars. It was now well into November, and their snow-covered clothes and scant blankets provided no real protection from the freezing cold.

Hungry and exhausted, Jouzas shivered as he staggered into the open boxcar with old Ruzvycius and his wife. They had survived so much. Now they rumbled through pelting snow in a cattle car full of haggard strangers to a dark unknown.

Finally, the train slowed and came to a stop. None of the German guards came to get them. They were abandoned without food or shelter in an underground train yard in the middle of Berlin.

The Reich had established specific locations as holding places for displaced persons from the occupied nations, and the Nazis deliberately funneled Baltic refugees into Berlin.

Russian bombs were falling everywhere, and everywhere Jouzas looked, the city was on fire. Day after day, Jouzas watched the surrounding buildings catch fire and collapse around them.

In the midst of the fire and falling buildings, old man Ruzvycius turned to his wife and said, "I need to go feed the horses." And he walked off of the train into the fiery night.

Jouzas watched him walk away and didn't try to stop him. They had been going without food and freezing and waiting for help for five days. Jouzas didn't know if he would die from hunger, fire, cold, or a bomb.

How would he survive this nightmare inferno? What was there to do? He could get off the train, but there was nowhere to go.

Baltic Refugees in a Cattle Car

Chapter 6

Refugee

"Help us," they cry. "Defend us against our enemies. Protect us from their relentless attack. Do not betray us now that we have escaped. Let our refugees stay among you. Hide them from our enemies until the terror is past." (Isaiah 16: 3-4)

Somehow Jouzas and Mrs. Ruzvycius survived the Berlin inferno, but they never saw the old man again.

After the torment of uncertainty in the train station, the bombing and fires subsided, and the Nazis came back and loaded Jouzas and Mrs. Ruzvycius on a train heading to Bavaria.

They were going to a place called Föhrenwald located in the town of Feldebine. It was one of over 100 German Displaced Persons (DP) Camps organized by nationality.

DP-Camp Föhrenwald was a converted German navy base now designated for the

3300 old people and children from Lithuania, Estonia, and Latvia who were arriving there by the trainload.

When Jouzas stumbled off the train, dizzy from hunger and fatigue, he was puzzled by a strange sight.

The refugees' filthy and soot-blackened clothes appeared to be covered with a white material that inexplicably undulated and changed designs as he looked. Then the realization struck him; their clothes were covered with lice.

The Germans had prepared for this, and they corralled everyone into a large disinfectant chamber and barked orders at the refugees to undress.

As Jouzas and the others stood naked and shivering, the Germans sprayed him down and drenched him with chemicals, making his eyes sting and his skin burn.

Then they marched Jouzas to another room where a guard shoved a different set of clothes into his arms. He hurriedly pulled them on, still coughing and sputtering, and searched for Mrs. Ruzvycius in the crowds of huddled people.

He found her, and the soldiers herded them into a crowded building with only four walls, no beds, or anything else except for hundreds of old people and children.

Many of the refugees were sick and diseased—infected from the fleas and lice that continued to infest the camp. They had no bathrooms, just latrines, and the whole camp smelled so bad that people could smell it from miles away.

Soldiers guarded the camp, surrounded by barbed wire. It was to be Jouzas' home for the next three months.

Germans who lived nearby, despite their own wartime trials and hardships, tried to find a way to care for the wretched refugees. Two German women came every day with big barrels of rutabaga soup.

Each day, Jouzas would take whatever container he could find and get in line with all the other refugees and wait for the soup to arrive. He hungrily held out his container and received his daily ration of one ladle of soup per day--day after day.

Jouzas was not sure how he and the thousands of other refugees in the sprawling camp could make it through the brutal

winter without heat and so little to eat. Some
of the sick began to die. Jouzas thought
maybe the chemical shower was responsible
for killing more than just lice and fleas.

A miserable Christmas passed with no
word from his family. Jouzas was always cold
and always hungry, but somehow, he made
it through the winter, and he promised
himself that if he survived, he would never
eat another rutabaga!

Then, In March, the Nazis ordered a
group of refugees, including Jouzas and Mrs.
Ruzvycius, to board a train that would take
them to Schleswig, a DP Camp on an inlet on
the sea in northern Germany close to
Denmark.

Jouzas didn't care. Life couldn't get
much worse, he thought, but he was wrong.
Mrs. Ruzvycius got sick, and in just a few
days, she died. Jouzas had lost his last
connection to home. As they pulled into
Schleswig, he was alone.

The Nazis ordered the refugees to get
off the train. Then, the Nazis got on the train,
and the refugees watched the train pull off
and leave them there. Jouzas found himself

on his own, desperately lonely and full of despair. He was eleven years old.

His new home was with 200 other displaced persons in one big building with four walls, no beds, and no one else around. In this camp, too, everyone suffered from fleas and lice.

The camp was open. No barbed wire and no soldiers were needed to keep them from leaving because there was nowhere for them to go. And there were no German caretakers coming with soup. They were on their own.

However, Jouzas thanked God when an old woman taking care of five children took pity on the lonely boy and took him in under her wings and began to look after him. For three months, they would be his substitute family in their temporary home.

Jouzas realized that if he was going to live, he must eat, but he had no food and no money. Then he had an idea. He and the children went out to the highway and looked gathered all the discarded cigarette butts they could find.

They carefully salvaged all the dregs of remaining tobacco. Once they gathered all they could find that day, they took the tobacco and traded it for a potato and eagerly divided it. The next day, they began earlier and found more butts. A man gave them a whole loaf of bread for their tobacco.

The days went on like this, searching for tobacco and trading it for food. If someone just took their tobacco and gave them nothing, they went hungry.

Often, Jouzas had no choice but to go to nearby German farmers and beg for food. They usually found a way to give him something, a potato or a piece of bread. One particular farmer pitied the small boy and always found something to give him to eat.

Jouzas tried to find other sources of food, but too often, he had to return to the old farmer's door, hoping that he would feed him one more time. Each time, the farmer managed to have enough food to share.

Thanks to the farmer, Jouzas and his little wartime family managed to scrape by and survive for the next two months until the war ended on May 8, 1945. Schleswig-Holstein became part of what was now the British zone, and Jouzas found himself on the way to another camp.

Föhrenwald Displaced Persons Camp

Klingsberg, the orphanage established in
Lübeck for Lithuanian children--and Jouzas'
home from 1946-1949

Chapter 7

God's Little Birds

"He defends the cause of the fatherless and the widow, and loves the foreigner residing among you, giving them food and clothing."
(Deuteronomy 10:18)

The war was over, and Jouzas was one of approximately 60,000 survivors of the 250,000 refugees--the farmers, tradesmen, and educated professionals who left Lithuania during the war.

As a nationality, Lithuanians were unusually healthy which perhaps helped them to survive near starvation and horrible conditions.

All refugees were called Displaced Persons or DPs, but the Lithuanians took the initials, DP, and called themselves "Dievo Pauksteliai" which translates to "God's Little Birds."

Like birds blown off course without a nest to call their own, the storms of war had blown them all far from home, and none of them knew if they could ever safely return to Lithuania or find a place to call home.

Not only did God's Little Birds endure deprivation, they also had to bear the suspicions of the Allies who thought that Lithuanians must have been Nazi sympathizers since they did not want to return to Lithuania.

After conducting official investigations over an extended period of time, the Allies finally realized that Lithuanians were war victims who had barely survived the brutality of both Nazi and Soviet occupation.

They feared that if they returned to a Soviet-ruled Lithuania, they would face the very execution or deportation to Siberia they had fled. History has proven that they were right.

As it turned out, most who ended up in Germany during WWII would not be returning home. They spent years in one of 113 DP camps under the care of the United Nations Relief and Rehabilitation Administration (UNRRA) until they emigrated to other countries in the late 1940's and early 1950's.

Jouzas was one of them. By now, twelve-year-old Jouzas spoke German and Russian in addition to Lithuanian, and he was able to follow the news and rumors passed among the adults in the camp.

He eagerly listened to any talk of post-war efforts to help people locate their families. But it would be a long time before life would resume a form of normalcy.

It would be even longer before Jouzas would get word of home, nor could he relax and feel that he was completely out of danger.

Word came from Allied officials that Jouzas and other Baltic refugees would be transported temporarily to an army base in Lübeck in the Holstein area of northern Germany.

They would stay there in the army barracks until they were housed more permanently in another DP camp nearby under British supervision, a former German navy base on the Baltic sea.

Jouzas did not want to board a ship being sent to Neustadt Bay. Rumors had been raging for months about numerous disasters that had befallen refugees while on ships on the Baltic Sea.

Just weeks earlier, two helpless ships loaded with refugees sank in Neustadt Bay after being attacked, according to one account, by the Germans.

Other, more terrible rumors told a different story, that in actuality, British fighter-bombers had bombarded and sunk the unarmed *Cap Arcona* and the *Thielbek* which were flying large white flags.

The gruesome stories also claimed that the British continued to fire on rescue boats filled with freezing and terrified survivors.

Of the nearly 9,000 souls on the two ships, most burned to death or drowned in the cold sea. Only 350-500 survivors were rescued from the fierce and brutal attack.

Adding even more fuel to his nightmares, Jouzas heard news of Soviet submarines torpedoing and sinking three other non-military ships on the Baltic Sea. In January, they sank the *Wilhelm Gustloff*, and over 5000 women and children perished.

In February, the *General Steuben* sank after being torpedoed, taking the lives of 3,500 refugees and wounded soldiers.

Worst of all, in April, a month earlier, 7000 refugees and wounded soldiers on the *Goya* were sent to deep, icy graves after being deliberately attacked by Soviet submarines.

Despite his fears, Jouzas reached Lübeck safely. The British had taken over the German concentration camp there. They converted it into a holding camp designated specifically for orphans who had come from German-occupied Baltic countries.

The British worked with UNRRA to distribute food and bring in workers to teach and care for the orphans. UNRRA had only 2500 workers to care for more than a million refugees in over 113 camps, 50,000 of whom were Lithuanians.

In this camp, the UNRRA woman in charge wisely decided to organize the children by nationality. In their DP camps, Lithuanian refugees organized the care and education of the Lithuanian children and orphans.

Lithuanian teachers not only took on the care of the orphaned children, they also continued the children's education in the Lithuania way, teaching them about Lithuanian culture and traditions and encouraging them to be proud of their nationality.

They accomplished this despite appalling working conditions, poor food and housing, and hardly any educational materials.

In Lübeck, the orphanage they established for the Lithuanian children was named Klingsberg--where for the next three years, Jouzas lived, attended school, and worked.

In 1946, UNRRA, the Lithuanian Red Cross, the Catholic Church, and the British Army worked hard to establish records for all the children, workers, and teachers in Lübeck to help people locate their families.

Jouzas didn't have any identification that could help them in their efforts, and to make their search even more hopeless, the Russians had sealed off borders and cut off communication.

After a year of concerted effort, they hadn't found a trace of Jouzas' family. He couldn't go home if they couldn't find his family. He had clung to the hope that his family managed to stay alive, but now he had no doubt that they were all dead.

They couldn't have survived the bombing, and even if they had, they would have had to cross through fields that surrounded their homes which were filthy with land mines.

It was terrible to accept, but Jouzas had to face the reality that he was truly an orphan without a home, and if his family wasn't alive, he didn't want to go back.

When he began to be overcome with despair, Jouzas stopped and thought about the many times his life had been spared, and he was thankful. He had always felt God with him, protecting him.

He felt grateful to have a place to live, and he worked hard at his assigned chores in the camp. He stopped uselessly hoping to find his family. He gave up trying to find a way to go home, and he began to settle into life in the camp.

Christmas 1946 came, and Jouzas fervently hoped that he would get a soccer ball. His excitement grew as he watched other boys open their gifts and pull out sporting equipment and soccer balls. He couldn't wait to open his.

He tore off the wrapping, and he couldn't believe his eyes. Instead of the longed-for ball, he pulled out a *doll*. He couldn't hide his disappointment, and he cried.

However, his disappointment didn't last long. Somewhere, somehow, someone found a ball, and it soon belonged to Jouzas.

He made friends in the camp, and they found time to have fun. One time, they decided to spend their spare time building a sailboat and spent many happy, long hours working on it together until they finally felt it was ready to sail!

They excitedly planned the day of the launch and looked forward to a victorious afternoon of sailing. The time had come. It was a beautiful day, and they proudly took their boat to the water, climbed in, and left the shore.

They had only gone a little way from shore when water started rising under their feet, and the boat began to ride lower and lower in the water. Within minutes, they were swimming for shore.

As they watched their grand experiment sink to the bottom of the lake, their spirits didn't sink with it. They'd had a wonderful time dreaming and building the boat together, and they would just move on to their next project.

Professor Petros and Bertha Gauris, themselves Lithuanian refugees, helped to organize the school in Klingsberg where they taught Jouzas and took care of him.

On the outside, the camp was a plain, uniform compound of big block buildings, but the teachers and other refugees did everything they could to preserve their country's traditions and way of life.

Jouzas was thankful for the Gaurys, and he was relieved to finally continue the education he had briefly begun six years ago in Lithuania. He felt happy to be taught in his own language surrounded by other children speaking Lithuanian.

Remarkably, a former concentration camp in Lübeck, Germany, had been turned into a *British* DP orphanage where Jouzas was able to go to *Lithuanian* school and learn Lithuanian songs, play Lithuanian games, and learn the practice of Lithuanian trades.

In the meantime while Jouzas adjusted to his new life in the orphanage, UNRRA, the British Army, and the Catholic Church were working to settle refugees in England, France, South America, Canada, and the United States.

All of these countries would take in refugees if they had relatives or sponsors who would take responsibility for providing food and shelter for them.

Most refugees contracted with farmers who would pay their way over, and then the immigrant would work to pay off their passage.

One of the workers in the camp was an old man who liked to tell Jouzas all about America. He urged Joe,

"America is where you should go. Everyone has all the food they can eat in America."

Jouzas loved sausage, so he asked the old man,

> "All the food you can eat? What about sausage?"

The old man promised,

> "In America you can buy and eat as much sausage as you want."

Jouzas began having dreams about America and sausage.

As people located their families and returned home, camps began to close. Church workers asked Jouzas where he wanted to go when they closed his camp.

Jouzas thought about what the old gentleman told him about life in America and about all the sausage there. He said, "America. I want to go to America."

At this time, President Truman's directive on displaced persons mandated that officials do everything possible to help find homes for the European war orphans.

The result was the placement of nearly 1400 children including babies from many nationalities. However, three years passed, and still there was no word about Jouzas' request to go to America.

If a child was not adopted by a family, a sponsor had to sign a legally binding contract to provide food and shelter for the immigrant.

Finally, in September,1949, the church contacted Jouzas again and asked if he still wanted to go to America. A Lithuanian woman in Scranton, Pennsylvania had volunteered to take in the fifteen year old orphan and be his sponsor.

Peter and Bertha Gaurys and Jouzas, age 12,
Klingsberg camp, 1946

United Lithuanian Relief Fund of America Ad

Group shot at Klingsberg-- Jouzas is third
from the right on bottom row

Chapter 8

Immigrant

"...for he said, 'I have been a sojourner in a foreign land.' " (Exodus 2:22)

His last day in the camp was an emotional one. Jouzas said goodbye to the Gauryses and to his friends who had been his family for the past four years, and like the family he had lost during the war, he would probably never see them again.

On January 7, 1950, he boarded a plane for the first time in his life. As he took his seat and waited for the plane to take off on its long flight, his emotions were in turmoil.

He was leaving familiar places and routines to fly across the ocean far from his homeland to a new, strange place. He didn't speak English; he didn't know anyone in America, and he didn't have a dime in his pocket.

He was also eager and grateful. He'd heard what everyone said about America, and he'd seen the movies. Everyone wanted to go to America, and now he, Jouzas, the orphaned hawk-fighter and cow-herder from Lithuania, was on a plane taking him there.

America was a country of educated, good-looking young people. It was the land of opportunity where you were free to work to follow your dreams.

Everyone was healthy in America; everyone could find work, and everyone had plenty to eat. Everyone lived in nice homes; everyone played sports; every child went to school and had the chance to go to college.

His anticipation and tension kept him awake. Finally, after an entire day of flying, the plane landed, and Jouzas gathered his few belongings, got off with the others, and took his first steps on American soil.

He was impatient to get settled in his new home and meet his sponsor, Mrs. Savage, the lady from Scranton who offered to take him in. How would he know her? How would she find him?

He wondered if she was out there right now in the sea of people surrounding him, waiting to greet him and take him home to Scranton.

To his surprise, he was immediately shuttled from the plane and herded with all the other children onto a bus and taken to another holding camp.

His mind swirled, and he couldn't process all the strange sights as the bus wove its way in and out of the blaring horns and congested traffic of New York.

He was disoriented by the tumultuous maze they traveled. He was startled by the black faces he saw for the first time in his life in the stream of hundreds of Americans rushing past the bus windows.

The bus pulled up to a stop in front of a large, rather run-down building that was several stories tall and surrounded by other buildings in the middle of an area of the city they called the Bronx.

It had been a YMCA building, but it had been abandoned during the war and hadn't been used until the orphans started arriving from Europe.

It was in need of repair and paint, inside and out. The rooms were small and dark, and the forty to fifty children were crowded into bedrooms on every story with a few bathrooms they all shared.

Jouzas gazed out the dirty window and saw concrete, asphalt, and barbed wire. This wasn't any better than Lubeck. He fought to keep from crying as disappointment washed over him.

Jouzas was one of the last waves of children who came through this Bronx orphanage. They came from all over Europe and included hollow-eyed Jewish children who spoke what Jouzas knew was Yiddish.

Jouzas tried to pick out languages from the noisy babble. He was able to decipher Russian, German, a little Polish, some French, and even the less familiar English. His spirits lifted when he finally heard a few children speaking Lithuanian.

A month passed, and Jouzas was still waiting to learn when he would finally leave the orphanage and meet his sponsor, but the people in charge couldn't tell him how long he was going to have to wait.

It was hard for him to sit around waiting and do nothing, and he particularly didn't like not having any money. He looked

around at the dilapidated building and got
an idea.

He went to the adults in charge and
told them he'd like to paint the house. After
a brief conference, one of the men said, "All
right. We'll pay you 10 cents an hour."

Jouzas got to work. He painted every
day for the next three months, and by the
time he finished the job, he had earned the
unheard-of sum of $30.

He wanted to make a good impression
when he met Mrs. Savage. He bought an $18
suit, so she would be glad she took on the
responsibility of sponsoring such a
respectable young man.

Then he had another idea. Why
should he keep waiting for someone to
make arrangements for him? He had more
painting money left. He could go to the bus
station and buy himself a ticket to Scranton
and find Mrs. Savage himself.

Jouzas got his belongings from the
orphanage and put on his suit. He found the
bus station and managed to make someone
understand that he wanted to go to

Scranton. He paid for his ticket and got on the bus.

After an eight-hour bus ride, he arrived in Scranton. He got directions to Mrs. Savage's address and walked to her house.

When Mrs. Savage, a Lithuanian in her 60's, opened the door, Jouzas stood there in his suit and introduced himself in Lithuanian.

She was surprised to see him, but quickly welcomed him and introduced him to her son, a carpenter who lived with her and worked in a bowling alley.

Mrs. Savage showed Jouzas where he would sleep, and when they sat at supper that night, she explained that Jouzas would need to find a job right away and contribute part of his pay to the household.

She also expected him to help with chores and the upkeep of the house. Jouzas nodded his agreement. He was in his new home, and he was being treated like a grown man. He would have to earn his keep.

Jouzas walked back to the Greyhound bus station the next day and quickly got a job washing dishes for 50 cents an hour.

The dishes would be piled up waiting for him when he arrived at 4:00pm and keep piling up all night while he washed. He worked hard, without taking a break, all night until all the dishes were washed around midnight.

One night, the cook shouted out an order to Jouzas, "Go to the freezer and bring me some hot dogs right away!" Jouzas dutifully left the dishes and hurried to the freezer.

He looked around everywhere, but he couldn't find them and had to return empty-handed. The cook angrily marched him back to the freezer and grabbed the hot dogs, right in front of his face.

Then it dawned on him that Jouzas had never heard of a hot dog. The cook had a good laugh over the horrified Lithuanian immigrant looking for the poor dogs thrown in the freezer to be chilled and ready to eat.

Jouzas worked all of the time. Every day, Mrs. Savage had a long list of tasks for Jouzas to complete at her house. She wanted him to paint this and fix that.

Jouzas didn't want Mrs. Savage to have any regrets about taking him into her home, so any time when he wasn't working his full-time job, he painted her house until he had painted it all inside and out.

He learned how to repair everything that needed fixing, making mistakes, and doing it over again until she was satisfied that he had done it right.

He worked either washing dishes at the bus station or doing chores for Mrs. Savage for five months, and then he met a Lithuanian man who worked at Currie Arts Plastics.

The Lithuanian man told him that the Jewish owner was hiring workers to carve plastics, and the pay was okay. Jouzas got a job making 75 cents an hour carving designs in perfume bottles.

The owner promised that if Jouzas got good at it, he would give him a raise. Jouzas practiced and practiced, and he did get good at it, but when he asked about his raise, the owner said,

"I can't raise your pay now, Jouzas; I don't have the money."

Surprised, Jouzas insisted, "You promised. Others are making $1.25 an hour. You pay, or I quit. "

The owner replied, "We'll see. Come back next week."

The next week, Jouzas asked again, but the owner still refused to increase his pay. Jouzas had too much pride to give in, so he gave his notice. Then he went home and prayed that he would be able to find a decent job by the end of the two weeks.

Jouzas received the answer to his prayer when a letter arrived addressed to him. Ever since he had left Lübeck the year before, he had faithfully stayed in touch with his teachers and friends, Bertha and Peter Gaurys.

The Gaurys, who didn't have children, had formed a close bond with the orphaned Jouzas. Jouzas eagerly opened the letter.

The Gaurys were delighted to share the great news that they, too, had successfully immigrated to America and were now living in Brooklyn in "Little

Lithuania" where there were Lithuanian bakeries, meat markets, and churches.

They lived in a two-bedroom apartment on the second floor of a block of buildings with plenty of room for Jouzas. How would he like to leave Scranton and come live with them?

Jouzas didn't hesitate. He said thank you and goodbye to Mrs. Savage and left Scranton as soon as he could make the arrangements.

He returned to New York and joyfully reunited with the Gaurys. It didn't take him long to find a new job. He was hired by Sullivan's Cabinet Shop in Rego Park in Queens, and he got that raise he had been hoping for--starting pay was $1.25 an hour.

Time out for a little fishing, Scranton, PA, 1950

Reunited in New York with Bertha and Peter
Gaurys, 1951

Part Three:
Putting Down Roots

Chapter 9

United States Airman

"You therefore must endure hardship as a good soldier of Jesus Christ." (2 Tim:2:3)

Life was good in America with the Gaurys, and over the next two years, Jouzas happily adjusted to American life and being a part of the thriving, hard-working immigrant community of "Little Lithuania" in the Bronx.

Jouzas worked hard and learned cabinetry skills at Sullivan's' cabinet shop. Then, six months after his 18th birthday, Jouzas received a letter from the United States Selective Service.

The notification informed Jouzas that as an adult male resident of the United States, he must register for service. The United States was actively deploying troops to support South Korea and Western Allies in the Korean Conflict .

Jouzas knew chances were good that he would be deployed to help fight off the Soviet-backed communists of North Korea.

He would be proud to serve his new country against the communists.

He thought it would be a good idea to join the Air Force. He noticed that the Air Force was full of good-looking, healthy people, and he could picture himself in a sharp, blue uniform.

So in March 1953, Jouzas signed his name as "Joseph Stasiukaitis" on an official United States document and became a United States Airman.

He said goodbye again to Bertha and Peter Gaurys and took one of two loaded chartered buses to Sampson Air Force base in Geneva, New York where he would undergo basic training.

On his bus, he met Tony Squicciarini who called him, "Joe." The two new airmen struck up a quick friendship. When they arrived in Geneva, the March wind blowing off the lake was damp and very cold.

Joe looked around in disappointment at the other newly enlisted airmen milling around the camp. They were an unattractive jumble of average-looking people in dirty clothes, not the fit Airmen of the sharp, blue uniforms he had seen in the advertisements.

On the third day of boot camp, Joe's drill sergeant shouted at the men,

"In the morning, we will start drilling. Has anyone ever drilled?"

Joe eagerly raised his hand, and as he looked around, he was proud to see that he was the only one who raised his hand. He smiled to himself about how lucky he was to be the only guy who had ever held a drill before and boasted,

"I used a drill many times in the cabinet shop where I worked."

Then to his shock, the Sergeant threw off his hat, stomped over, and grabbed him by his collar:

"I've got a wise guy! What's your name?"

"J-Joe Stasiukaitis, sir."

"Okay Poncho, meet me in the latrine."

By 10:00 p.m., everyone was in bed, except Joe. As he polished the brass in the latrine, he tried to figure out what he had done to make the sergeant mad. He finally crawled into bed around midnight.

The next day, he learned what a drill was. And he learned that he wasn't very good at it. That night, he polished the brass in the latrine again.

Latrine duty became Joe's routine. He couldn't stay in step, and his missteps would hold up the flight of 72 men. The Sergeant would chew Joe out and threaten him, shouting, "Poncho, you will NEVER make it three months!"

The sergeant tried marching Joe in front. He marched him in the middle, and he marched him in the back; but no matter where Joe was or how hard he tried, he never could stay in step.

Night after night, Joe polished the brass in the latrine. He was relieved that the others were asleep by the time he came to bed and didn't see his eyes red from crying.

Even getting dressed was a challenge for Joe. Before the first day of marching, each man was given a one-piece fatigue uniform. They were out of any uniforms that might fit the compact, short young man and issued Joe an extra-large uniform.

When Joe put on his uniform, the pants legs were way too long. He quickly cut two feet off and hurriedly shuffled out to march with the crotch of his uniform hanging down to his knees.

His hat was too big, too, and whenever the drill sergeant got frustrated with Joe, which was often, he stalked over to Joe and yanked his hat down past his ears.

Sometimes the drill sergeant asked for volunteers for certain detail work. Joe's "friend," Tony Squicciarini, knew that Joe still had trouble with English, so he would make sure that Joe understood what the sergeant had said.

"The sergeant is giving away a free weekend pass, Joe," Tony would whisper. "Raise your hand!" After Joe finished the volunteer detail, he usually wrapped up his day with latrine duty.

Every day was the same: waddle out in his ill-fitting uniform, struggle to march in step, sweat over the assigned detail, and polish the latrines.

Like all airmen, Joe was required to keep his shoes polished and ready for inspection under his bed. Joe tried hard to meet these expectations, but sometimes he was too exhausted to even remember to polish them before he fell into bed.

His friend, Tony, suggested that he rotate his shoes. Joe wasn't sure what that meant; he only had one pair of shoes that he wore every day. He figured out that it meant he should wear the left shoe on the right foot and the right shoe on his left.

The Sergeant took one look at Joe, and it was back to latrine-duty. Joe spent three months in boot camp. He had extra duty nearly every day, and he spent two nights out of three polishing the latrine.

Every night as Joe polished the brass, he swore to himself that if he ever made it out of boot camp, he would find a way to get back at that drill instructor.

To his relief and everyone else's surprise, Joe completed boot camp. His first assignment was to serve as a building engineer in Montana.

After being stationed in Montana for a month, Joe received his orders to go to Korea . Joe had a week of leave before he shipped over to Korea, so he went home to spend time with the Gaurys in New York.

When he left them again, he went to Parks Air Force base in California and boarded the *General Walker*, that left the dock at San Francisco to carry 6000 new United States airmen to their first stop in Yokohama, Japan.

The weather was terrible, and Joe got KP duty again; but for once, it was a blessing. KP duty was in the bottom of the ship where it was cool, and Joe didn't get seasick despite the heaving seas.

All of the other 6000 wretchedly seasick men lived through seven days of indescribable mess and stench, tossing in their canvas bunks with only sixteen inches between them.

Once Joe reached Yokohama, he flew to Busan East (K-9) Air Base and from there on to Kunsan (K-8) Air Base on the west coast of the South Korean peninsula bordered by the Yellow Sea.

Seven months later in February 1953, Joe made a 55-mile trip up the Nakdong River to another camp, Taegu (K-2).

It would be here, nearly 5000 miles from his birthplace in Lithuania and about 7000 miles from his new home in America, that Joe, the United States Airman, would become a proud and dedicated United States citizen.

As an Air Force civil engineer, Joe's duty was to run the carpentry shop, and he was put in command of 27 Koreans. He had begun learning cabinetmaking at Sullivan's Cabinet shop, but in Korea, he got his real education in the cabinet-making industry.

He ran the shop all year and never had any problems, except for one. He was working on a joiner, a piece of equipment which has a rotating blade that cuts the wood as it is being pushed in under the sharp, spinning blade.

It's very dangerous, but it was the common method for woodworking. Joe was pushing in a piece of wood when the wood slipped, and the index finger of his right hand went under the blade.

It was September 1953. He was 19 years old, and he'd only been running the shop for a month. About a year later, he lost his second finger.

The winters were miserably cold, and ice would coat the pierced steel planks of the runway. Joe and his men maintained the runway by loading 2½ ton dump trucks with sand and sending two to four men out to cover the planks with sand in the freezing cold and blowing wind.

They'd listen to the radios for word of when the planes were coming in, so they could hurry and get off of the runway. Then they'd move back in as soon as the planes left and get back to work covering the iced-over planks with sand.

It was a tough duty, and even the base commander felt sorry for the men out in the freezing weather. He took two bottles of liquor to Joe to give to the men to keep them warm.

Another time, a lieutenant gave Joe and his men 20 bottles of liquor in exchange for 50 sheets of plywood so his marines could build more comfortable tents to keep out the cold.

Joe and his men took turns with guard duty, and the weather made this duty, already considered to be a rough one, even harder. Whoever was on duty had to stay alert all night, but Joe felt lucky that they had a building and a potbellied stove.

They heated the stove until the steel of the stove turned red. As they stood close to the stove to get warm, their front sides would scorch, but their backsides would freeze.

With the liquor that the commander and the lieutenant gave him, Joe threw a party at the plumbing shop for his men. Some of the airmen couldn't find their way back to their barracks and slept in the shop or wherever they could find a place to lie down.

Joe wasn't used to drinking, but the liquor made him feel warm. The next thing he knew, he was waking up with the feeling of water on his face. He was on the ground, and it was raining. He had fallen asleep in a foxhole.

One night, Joe was patrolling by himself and walking the perimeter. Once again, it was raining and cold, and Joe was wearing his big coat and two pairs of pants. Suddenly, he heard a loud "pow," and then he found himself in a hole.

He wasn't sure what had happened, but he thought that maybe someone had knocked him on the head, and he had fallen into the hole. He still had his rifle on his shoulder, cocked and ready. He was never able to solve this mystery.

(*A little over sixty years later, Joe's grandson, Brian, travelled to Korea and went to Kunsan to find the carpentry shop and air strip that Joe and his men had guarded and covered with sand. All that remained were fields of rice paddies.*)

Finally, the war ended in 1954. Joe came back to the United States and got stationed at Beale Air Force base, formerly a pilot training base in WWII, north of Sacramento, California.

During the war, the service branches were often mixed together, and after the war, Joe was put under engineering command with the army of engineers.

Joe was assigned to the 8802nd engineering battalion under the command of Captain Cottma, a smart, no-nonsense, and well-respected leader.

By now, the services were desegregated, and Joe had grown more accustomed to seeing black people. He and the other engineers respected and liked Captain Cottman, a black man.

The training base had 84,000 acres of land, and their work was to go out to where the training took place and replace the many rotten wooden bridges with concrete.

This was a big job, and it took over a year to complete. When Joe realized how many bridges there were, he thought, "Let's just blow them up. We'll just dynamite them on the first day."

They did dynamite some bridges. At first, the bridges appeared to rise up, and then they fell down. But for the most part, two men had to go in at a time and take down the bridges by hand with a 6-8 foot blade chainsaw.

Joe and another man went to the top of the first bridge and started the chain saw. The next thing he knew, he had been flipped off the bridge and was flying through the air. As he landed in a ditch, he thought, "Well, I'm supposed to be showing them how to do it."

Sometimes they had to dig a runway and then cover it back up. Other days, they had to cut trees down and clear the land completely, all part of the training.

Three days a month, they went into the field for training and had to pitch their tents and live on c -rations.

Joe noticed that the many people stationed there with him didn't understand much English, at least the way he spoke it. He would give them instructions, and they would say, "Don't understand. Don't understand."

Unfortunately, there were a lot of people who didn't understand Joe's instructions, and there was a lot of work that Joe had to find a way to get done without their help.

In April 1955, Joe got his new assignment to go to Charleston, SC. Joe had two more years to finish his active service and four years of reserves. After that, Joe would receive the citizenship papers he had signed in Taegu, South Korea.

Joe knew that some of his fellow servicemen had gone to Charleston after the war, so he was looking forward to Charleston, but once again, Joe was disappointed.

One of his first disappointments was learning that McCutcheon, his roommate, could not go to places in town where Joe could go. Joe couldn't even leave the base with his roommate.

This was a shock to Joe, and he felt bad for his black roommate. To make matters worse, Joe became uncomfortable rooming with McCutcheon who was getting angrier and angrier over the situation.

Once, in a terrible mood, McCutcheon jumped on Joe. Bruce, another airman from Georgia, grabbed a door off of its hinges to come between them.

Joe wasn't sure he wanted to stay in Charleston. When Joe had leave, he went to see the Gauryses who had plans to move to Palm Beach. On the other hand, it wasn't bad living and working on the Charleston base.

He met Dwayne McCubbin, and the two became good friends. He worked in a cabinet and carpentry shop on the base, and it felt good to be doing work where he had so much competence.

He looked forward to the military parades every Saturday with the band and brass and flying flags. Joe added up all the reasons for going with the Gauryses or staying in Charleston. He had a good friend, decent housing, satisfying work, and parades on Saturday. He decided to stay.

United States Air Force Airman
Joseph Stasiukaitis

US citizen Joseph Stasiukaitis receives his
naturalization papers, May 25, 1954

102

Chapter 10

Building a Home

"Behold, children are a heritage from the Lord, the fruit of the womb, a reward. Like arrows in the hand of a warrior are the children of one's youth. Blessed is the man who fills his quiver with them! He shall not be put to shame when he speaks with his enemies in the gate." (Psalm 127:3-5)

After eleven years of being sent from camp to camp in Germany, shuttling back and forth from New York to Pennsylvania, and then being moved from base to base in Korea, Joe had settled into life on an Air Force base in Charleston, South Carolina.

He had survived WWII, spent his youth as an orphan, served his new country in a foreign war, mastered a trade, and fulfilled what once had been an impossible dream: he became a United States Citizen.

He had a lot to be thankful for. His work in the cabinet shop on the base was going well, and he had buddies there. But in all these years, he never felt that he had a place he could call home to replace the one he had lost as a ten year old boy.

If he could find someone to love, he could marry and start a family. He would have a family of his own to help fill the lonely place in his heart that had been there ever since he lost his mother and family in the war. So far, he hadn't met anyone.

One day after work, Joe and his buddy headed to Target, his favorite drive-in restaurant on the corner of Highway 52 and Remount Road, to grab a barbecue sandwich. And then he saw her.

A pretty slim girl with brown hair, not quite as tall as he was at 5'5" skated up to the car to take their order, Joe smiled at her, and she smiled back.

"What's your name?"
"Ruth."
"Do you live here?"
"No, I'm just here visiting my brother. I came to see him and go to the ocean."
"Where does your brother live?"
"On the air base."
"Really? I live on the air base, too. What's his name?"

"Roy Wheeler."

"Sergeant Wheeler, the cook?"

"Yes, he's in charge of the mess."

"I know him! How long are you
staying?"

"Just for the summer. I have to go
back home to finish high school."

"Where's home?"

"Baxter, Tennessee."

"Where's your home?"

"The air base."

"No, silly, where are you really from?"

"Lithuania."

"Oh!"

And it went on from there. He teased
her, and she teased him back, and they
made arrangements to meet again the next
evening at the drive-in.

They met each other night after night
at the drive-in, and he and Ruth would laugh
and tease and flirt. Joe enjoyed her sense of
humor, and she had the kind of friendly, nice
personality he liked.

Joe could tell that she cared for him,
too. When it was time for Ruth to return to

Tennessee, they promised each other they would write, and they did.

They wrote each other for a year. Joe missed her and decided that letters weren't enough. He needed to go to see her as soon as he could get leave.

Joe reached the small town of Baxter in the hills of Tennessee and found Ruth's home, an old house in the country with chickens scratching in the yard and horses looking at him curiously over the barbed wire fence next to the house.

Ruth and her mother greeted him at the door and invited him in. Her mother invited him to stay for supper, and then she returned to the kitchen to finish preparing the meal on their pot-bellied stove.

Joe and Ruth made a little polite talk and then fell quiet. Eventually Ruth excused herself to go help her mother. Joe sat and looked around at their home.

The house wasn't wired for electricity, but a wire was strung from a pole with a meter on it that came into the house and was attached to a pull chain that looped from one light to another.

Joe washed up by using a hand pump to pump the water into the house that drained out into a ditch by the house.

At supper, they talked casually about his life at the Air Base, Ruth's brother who was starting a restaurant in Charleston, and Joe's trip up to Tennessee. After supper, Joe and Ruth walked outside alone.

Soon, they ran out of things to say. Eventually, Ruth broke the awkward silence. While they were apart, she began, she had met someone, but she quickly went on to say that they had broken up, and she was very happy to see Joe.

She had really missed him. There was only one problem, and it cast a dark shadow over what should have been a happy reunion. Ruth was pregnant.

Joe tossed and turned all that sleepless night. He thought about his dream of a home and family. He thought he loved Ruth, and he knew she needed him. They had fun together, and she obviously cared for him. He prayed about what to do.

Joe blamed himself. If he had come to see her sooner, this would not have happened. If they had been together, she would not have looked at anyone else.

He had a good job on the base, and he could provide a home for Ruth and her baby in Charleston. Hadn't his own mother raised three children who were not her own? He could do it, too. They would be a family.

So in 1956, 23 year old Joe, who had remained a faithful Catholic, and sixteen year old Ruth, who didn't belong to any church, got married by a priest in a Catholic ceremony, just as Joe hoped they would.

Ruth moved to Charleston with Joe, and they set up their home on the Air Force base. Baby Anna soon joined them. A year later, Ruth was pregnant again with Joe's first baby, and Joe decided it was time to get out of the military.

He needed to find a home for his growing family. He bought a lot on Butler Street off of Rivers Avenue, close to the base where he would be working as a civil servant, and he worked with a contractor to build a house for his family.

The contractor framed in the house, and Joe finished it off. Baby Lola came along in the spring of 1958, and the next year, his first son Robert was born. In 1960, they had another little girl, Kathy, and a few years later, in 1963, Paul joined the family.

Life was busy and noisy with five little children. Joe realized they needed a bigger home, so he put their house on the market. To his satisfaction, they sold it for twice what it had cost to build it only six years earlier.

He took the money he made on the house and bought a lot on Live Oak Road in Summerville to build another house, big enough for his family of seven.

Joe worked on building his family a modern new split-level house. Half of the home was at one level above the entrance, and the other half was below the level of the entrance. Joe built the house himself and quickly framed it all in.

John and Gwen Wessinger, who had two children, Jerry and Julie, were building a house on a lot down the street. They often met over building their homes, and the two young families quickly became good friends.

One afternoon, shortly after he had gotten his family of four children and infant Paul settled in to their nearly completed home, Joe was finishing off the garage when Gwen came running over.

She rushed up to Joe, short of breath, and gasped out, "The President. Someone has shot President Kennedy."

Joe couldn't believe it. He put down his tools, and he went inside with Gwen to watch the news on the black and white television. As they stared at a black screen, they could hear Walter Cronkite's voice:

> "This is Walter Cronkite in our newsroom. There has been an attempt, as perhaps you know now, on the life of President Kennedy. He was wounded in an automobile driving from Dallas Airport into downtown Dallas, along with Governor Connally of Texas. They've been taken to Parkland Hospital where their condition is as yet unknown."

They waited impatiently to hear more and finally Cronkite continued,

> "We have not been told their condition. At Dallas, in a downtown hotel room, a group had been gathered to hear President Kennedy and was waiting his

arrival. Let's switch down there now where Eddie Barker of KRLD is on the air."

Time crawled, but after less than 40 minutes, Walter Cronkite's face came onto the screen, and he said in a voice that he had difficulty controlling,

"From Dallas, Texas, the flash apparently official, President Kennedy died at 1 p.m. Central Standard Time, 2 o'clock Eastern Standard Time, some 38 minutes ago."

Joe was sad to see this happen to his country, but there was nothing anyone could do. After a while, Joe went back to work on the garage and finished it.

He took his family to mass where they prayed with everyone else for the dead Catholic president and his family and for the country now in shock. Then he and Ruth and the children, like the rest of the country, went on with their lives.

Joe was deeply thankful that the Lord had watched over him, a terrified orphan, during that terrible time of the war, and that He had brought him to his new country where he lived in his own nice home, drove his own car, and had a good job.

Joe believed with all his heart that God had His hand on his life, and he never forgot what he had learned those years ago going with his father to the Cathedral in Pajevonys. Now he faithfully took his children to mass at St. John the Beloved in Summerville.

Attending was not an option for anyone in the family, and none of the seven of them ever missed. They went to Saturday evening mass every weekend, and sometimes they went again on Sunday.

It was always a struggle to get three little girls out of the door to arrive to mass on time, and often Ruth would grab Kleenex and pin it on the girls' heads at the last minute to abide by the rule of girls having their heads covered.

On Tuesdays, Joe sent the children to catechism. The children walked from school to the church for their lessons about the Catholic church and Jesus. If they misbehaved, they remembered that nuns could swing a mean ruler.

Joe had finished his four years of military service in 1957 and signed up for four years in the Reserves when he transitioned into work in the civil service.

When that commitment was fulfilled, he continued to serve in the National Guard, and every month he spent a weekend at McEntire Joint National Guard Base in Columbia, SC. Every year, he would be sent off somewhere for two weeks of active duty.

He worked hard to provide for his family. He worked constantly either at his job or in his side business framing houses and building cabinets out of his garage.

He rarely took time off, and he didn't have a lot of time to just enjoy being a father, but he worked hard so they would have what they needed, and so that Ruth could stay home with the children.

Money was tight, and Joe couldn't afford to take the family on vacation, but he found inexpensive ways to enjoy family time. After church they packed up a picnic and drove out to Folly Beach where the children romped and laughed in the surf and sand.

Joe had learned how to crab from John Wessinger. Ruth would come behind Joe with the net, and they would catch enough crabs so that a family day at the ocean came with dinner, too.

Sometimes they would drive up to see Ruth's family in Baxter just for the weekend. Joe would load up the car with plenty of food to feed everybody for at least a week. Ruth's family was always very happy to see them.

The children loved it because it felt like camping, and they loved their snuff-dipping grandmother and the horses and chickens.

Robert decided one time that he was going to learn to ride a horse, and after watching what the grownups did, he put a bit in a horse's mouth, got a hemp rope bridle, hit the horse on rump, and within two days had learned to ride.

Ruth's family was the only family Joe had, so he looked after them as a good son would, and if they were short on cash, he would find a way to come up with enough to help them get by.

Joe became good friends with Ruth's brother Roy Wheeler in Charleston, and the two families spent time together. Joe often took the family out to the North 52 Drive In and La Brasca's Pizzeria, opened and run by his brother-in-law.

Sometimes Ruth would take them out for pizza at the Pizzeria, and then she would put blankets over the children and go to the drive in. Once they were inside the arena, the children would pop out from under the blankets and watch the movie.

The children looked forward to seeing their aunt and uncle and to playing with cousin Bobby who was around Anna's age. They also experienced the sorrow of watching Bobby slowly die of cancer when he was only 10 years old.

What made it worse was that Uncle Roy gave Joe Bobby's clothes to give to his sons. Practical as always, Joe told Robert, who was Bobby's size, to wear them. Every day Robert shuddered as he put on his dead cousin's clothes and prayed that he would hurry and outgrow them.

The Stasiukaitis family loved living next door to the Wessinger's. Mrs. Wessinger always had cookies or a treat ready for them, and Mr. Wessinger called everyone "Honey."

Mr. Wessinger's good friend, J. W. Long, had a cabin on the Edisto River. They often went there together to enjoy it and invited the Stasiukaitis family to come too.

Going to the little cabin on the river became a highlight of their growing-up years. Joe would take the family there and pitch a tent for them by the cabin. Everyone ate together in the open-air eating area.

J. W. had a sock seine net, and he, John Wessinger, John's son-in-law Pat, and Dwayne McCubbin, Joe's friend from the service, took turns taking the boat out in groups of three several times a weekend.

Two men pulled the seine, and one man stayed in the boat. When they operated the sock seine net, they couldn't let the top of the net get low, or they would lose all their catch.

6'3" Dwayne and 5'5" Joe were nicknamed Laurel and Hardy, and they teamed up with John for their turn. John watched as Joe's head disappeared, and the pole bobbed along under the water. Joe's head popped back up, disappeared again, and popped up again.

They went up a creek at high tide, stopped on one side, and walked across with the net and held it down for about 20 to 30 minutes, and then they brought it back up together, full of fish, crab, and shrimp.

They dumped their catch in a big washtub and ran back to the landing, and the children and women would dump it into a big covered work area and sort it.

Sometimes they pulled up trash fish or dolphin or little sharks and threw them back into the water. Robert and Jerry caught little squid and played with them.

The Wessingers fried or sautéed shrimp, oysters, and fish. Everyone ate to their hearts' content. There was nothing like a freshly caught all-you-can-eat seafood dinner.

One of the few longer trips they made as a family was with the Wessingers to Stone Mountain, Georgia. They packed up all their camping gear and drove four and a half hours. They arrived at night and had to set up a big eight-man military tent.

Someone had smuggled beer on the trip. Mrs. Wessinger was a teetotaler, but Mr. Wessinger would slip over to Joe's to enjoy a beer together from time to time, and now seemed like a good time to enjoy one while Mrs. Wessinger was busy making supper.

They stealthily drank the beer while they were pitching the tent. It took a long time to pitch the tent.

Mrs. Wessinger, the inveterate cook, had plenty of time to prepare dinner, and she surprised them by managing to cook a pot roast on the exhaust manifold of the car.

One Christmas, the Wessingers invited Joe's family to come over to celebrate the holiday together. Mrs. Wessinger had made some very tasty scuppernong grape *juice* using a bottle and balloon the way Mr. Wessinger showed her.

Joe accepted the offered drink, downed the glass, raised his eyebrows, said, "Oh man, that's good!" and asked for a refill. Watching Joe pour himself some more, John winked and whispered so Gwen couldn't hear, "Don't drink it all! Save some for little winemaker me."

Despite working hard, Joe didn't have much money to spare, and he was thankful that he could go to the GEX, the Government Employee Exchange, and get a discount on groceries because he was in the Civil Service.

He and Ruth loaded the children up in Joe's 58 Chevy. The floorboards in the back were completely rusted through, so Joe covered the holes with plywood. The children could lift up the plyboard and watch the road rushing by.

When they pulled into the parking lot of the store, he admonished the three brothers and two sisters, "You stay here in the car and behave yourselves. We'll be right back." Then he and Ruth went inside the store to complete their shopping.

When they returned to the car, Joe studied the children for a moment. He took in their panting chests, red, sweaty faces, and hair sticking out all over the place. He quietly asked, "What's going on?" "Nothing," they replied in unison. He gave them a little smile and drove them home.

Every year they made two special trips to Sears in downtown Charleston near the Francis Marion Hotel to buy new clothes for Easter and for the start of school. Joe ushered all five children into the store.

Then he focused on outfitting one child while the other four occupied themselves, which to them meant freedom to run around.

Sears had a double tiered candy section that proved to be just too much temptation for the restless and unsupervised children.

They each grabbed up some candy and stashed it away. When they got back in the car, they all pulled out candy bags and started eating it.

Joe took one look at the purloined candy and took them right back into the store to return it and apologize. The four culprits boohooed and blubbered out that they were sorry and handed back the grubby, partially eaten candy.

The next time Joe brought them to Sears, he left them in the car while he took each one in, one at a time, while the others sat and waited, candy-less, in the car.

Joe believed in discipline, and he brought up his children with strict rules. They never missed mass on Sunday, and on Fridays, they always ate fish.

On summer and weekend mornings, five children running in and out of the house wasted a lot of air conditioning, so Joe would ask, "In or out?" If they said, "Out," they were sent outside and told to stay there. If they said "in" there was no changing their minds.

If they broke the rule and came in, Joe would yell, "You kids are letting all the air out!" They could come in for lunch, eat, and return outside where they would play all day.

Because they couldn't come back in, four-year-old Paul wasn't sure what he should do if he needed to use the bathroom. Robert told him with big brother authority, "Haven't you ever seen guys use a tree? It's okay if you can't go inside; just find a tree."

One day, Joe was inside reading the paper when he saw Paul "using" a tree next to the driveway. He ran out and grabbed Paul and spanked him.

Paul just looked at Joe and didn't say a word. Then when Joe went back to reading the paper, he ran around the house and found Robert and tackled him to the ground.

One of the lessons that Joe wanted to pass on to his children was the necessity of hard work in order to get ahead. He put them to work in his shop from the time they were six or seven years old.

Joe told them, I'm going to make you do something you don't have to do, but I'm going to pay you twenty-five cents to do it.

When Joe introduced Robert to his new chore of cleaning the shop on the weekends, Robert decided it was time to apply another lesson he had learned from watching his father.

He told his father that he had figured out that the chore was worth 50 cents. His father countered with, "I'll pay you 25 cents." Robert stood his ground.

His father had the final word: "I can make you clean the shop for free if I want to!" Robert quickly accepted the 25 cents.

Now that the children were older and in school, Ruth decided that she could go to work, too, and she and a friend started cleaning houses on the Air Base together when the children were in school.

Sometimes Joe would come home and find that Ruth wasn't there, and the children were at home by themselves or down the street at the Wessingers.

He wasn't happy about this, but they all seemed to be doing well at school, and Gwen Wessinger always welcomed them and made them feel at home, giving them something good to eat and helping them with their homework.

He shouldn't complain. Life was good. He had work and opportunity. Their children were thriving and getting educated, and they had good friends to enjoy time with at the river.

But everything was about to change.

Joe, Ruth, Paul, Anna, Lola, Robert, Kathy, 1965

Chapter 11

Rebuilding a Family

"For every house is built by someone, but God is the builder of everything." (Hebrews 3:4)

Joe read his new order from the Base Commander. Joe dutifully obeyed and reported to work in Bluffton, SC, although it was a two-hour drive from home.

He could come home only on Sundays when he would take his family to mass at St. Johns.   Joe didn't complain. He made the best of it, and he knew Ruth could take care of the children until this job was over.

Because of his new work location, he had an opportunity to invest in wild buffalos from Montana and brought four of them to Savage Island off of the coast of Bluffton.

Then one week, he was glad to be able to get away early and come home on a Saturday instead of a Sunday. When he arrived, Ruth wasn't there.

Joe found out that she had left the children with a family friend so she could go out with friends. He learned that she regularly went out whenever he was away.

Joe was dumbfounded and furious. His suspicions grew. He found it difficult to trust her and decided that the children could not be in the same house with her.

He ordered her to get out immediately. Ruth went to live with her brother, Roy, and his wife who were living in Pimlico, SC, about thirty minutes away.

After many days, Joe calmed down and thought it over. It was his fault. He was gone too much. He forgave her. He went to Pimlico and asked her to come home.

Ruth came home, and, despite the strain and the constant arguing and fighting, Joe thought they might work things out. But after some time had passed, he found a receipt that had fallen out of her pocketbook. It was signed, "Riley."

When Ruth got home that evening, she took one look at Joe and knew there was trouble. They lived through a terrible time of constant yelling and name-calling. The children huddled in their rooms crying.

One day after weeks of misery, Robert came upon his father sitting alone in a room crying. Once again, Ruth packed her things and left, but this time, it was for good.

Joe got full custody of all of the children, including Anna whom he had adopted. Joe had his hands full, and he tried to maintain the strict discipline that he had established before his marriage fell apart.

It was hard on all of them. How could he work all week, run his business, and raise five children all alone? Joe used the weekends to build cabinets and furniture to make more money, so the children had to maintain the home.

Every Saturday Joe would organize the children to clean up the house and keep up the yard, assigning them chores like doing dishes, vacuuming, and cutting the grass.

Joe was a little harder on the boys than he was on the girls. One Saturday, Kathy tearfully protested, "I work too hard. I want a day off." To Robert and Paul's shock, Joe said, "Go ahead. Go downstairs and take a day off."

Joe checked on her after a while, and she said, "Dad, I want a Pepsi." And Robert

128

and Paul watched in amazement as this imposter who *looked* like their father went away and came back with a Pepsi.

Despite all his efforts to keep everything going at home, the children got mad at Joe and, tired of his rules and chores, they called their mother to come get them.

Ruth and her new husband, who lived in a single-wide trailer in Marietta, Georgia, made the drive to pick up all five children who spent the summer in unsupervised freedom doing anything they wanted.

Then they got mad at their mother, and Joe made the drive to Georgia and brought them home. They eventually grew tired of Joe's rules again, and they left him once more to go back to the free life with his ex-wife and their stepfather.

After several times of moving them between households, Joe sat them down and declared, "You can stay with your mother or you can stay with me, but there will be no more back and forth. Your choice."

Anna did not want to leave her mother, and the other children didn't want to be apart. They broke Joe's heart and decided to stay with Ruth.

Robert who was nine when his parents divorced confided that their lives had become one of terrible upheaval and increasing uncertainty.

Their stable, predictable home in a community where they thrived was replaced by a life where they did not know where they would be on any given night. One time they moved to Tennessee in the middle of the night because the rent hadn't been paid.

They lived in Georgia, Florida, and Idaho. In Coeur d'Alene, Idaho, they saw snow for the first time and went fishing, but there and like so many other times, neither Ruth nor their stepfather was around.

They were put to bed on the floor in various houses, and Robert recalled that when he woke up, his first thought was to look for his mother and father, and then he remembered that his father wasn't there. Too often, he couldn't find his mother either.

With Ruth, money was tight, and they lived on welfare. Ruth took the children to the "Commodities" store to get basic necessities. Everything was stamped with the

US Army Surplus label, so there was no hiding the fact that they lived on assistance.

Robert had learned from his father the importance of being reliable and working hard to earn money. To help support the family, he got a job delivering papers and got himself up every morning to go out into the pre-dawn, bone-numbing, Idaho cold.

Many miles away, Joe was alone. He continued to work as hard as ever. He came home to an empty house that he had built for his wife and children with such love and hope, and he thought of his children living with Ruth--somewhere.

He still went to mass, but with a divorce looming ahead, how would he be able to continue going to church as though nothing had changed?

Joe prayed for answers, but it was a sad and lonely time. One terrible year had passed, then another, and in 1969, the divorce was final.

At the end of 1969, his friend Ed Rawls, a mechanical engineer at the Air Force Base, said, "C'mon Joe. You need to get out. Let's see in the new year at the New Year's Eve party at the Francis Marion Hotel!"

Joe agreed, and they drove to the grand old hotel in Charleston. After they got some drinks and stood around talking for a while, Joe looked around the ballroom at the young women standing in groups around the dance floor.

Joe singled out a pretty woman who looked nice standing with a group of women. He decided it was time to make his move and walked over to stand at her right side.

He tried to engage her in conversation, but she wouldn't acknowledge him or answer any of his questions. Finally Joe gave up and turned to Ed and complained, "She looks like a nice lady, but she's too stuck up to talk to me."

No sooner had he said this, she turned around and spoke in a concerned voice, "Were you talking to me by any chance? I ask because I'm afraid I might have missed something you said" She went on to explain, "I'm deaf in my right ear."

She introduced herself as Sara Henry, and Joe introduced himself, and they both laughed at how he had misjudged her. Soon they were having a good time laughing and dancing and talking. She even said, "I love your accent!" So Joe talked some more.

At the end of the dance, Sara told her friend. "He is such a gentleman. I'm going to let him take me home from the dance."

Joe drove Sara home to the apartment she shared with a college roommate across the Ashley River. He opened the car door for her and walked her to her door.

Then, he got up his courage and asked, "Sara, can I see you again?" Charmed by his good manners and European accent, Sara without hesitation replied, "Yes."

They started dating and learning more about each other. In addition to being pretty, Sara was likeable and made friends easily.

She had what Joe thought of as a normal American background and family, and she had been born in Georgia but had moved to Batesburg, South Carolina with her parents when she was in 11th grade.

She was an educated woman who had gone to Lander College in South Carolina and had studied library arts. One of the requirements of her scholarship was to work for three years in a state public library.

She completed that requirement in Spartanburg, and then she and a roommate decided to come to Charleston together where she found a job as a librarian at A.C. Corcoran Elementary school.

She was 30 years old. She learned that Joe was 36, and in his strong accent that she loved, he told her most of his life story.

He told her about fleeing Lithuania, surviving through the war alone, coming to America, joining the Air Force, serving in Korea, working on the Air Force Base, and about how he was working to fulfill his dream of having his own business.

He told her everything--or almost everything. He did not tell her he had been married, nor did he tell her he was the father of five children.

It wasn't long before Joe was thinking very seriously about Sara. She could be the one he was praying foe. He knew it was time to tell her everything.

He prayed the Lord would help him find the right time and the right words.

Finally, he got up the nerve and told her.
Sara simply said, "I'd like to meet them."

First, she met Robert, who had come
home for a visit, and they got along fine.
Then she met the other children. She wanted
them to like her so much that she decided
to cook for them for their first meeting.

In her nervousness, she burned the
fries. In dismay, she burst into tears. But she
had already won their hearts. They thought
Sara was a dream come true--just what they
thought a mother should be.

She was good looking with an
unusually sweet personality; she didn't
smoke or have any other bad habits; she had
already become good friends with Gwen
Wessinger; and she loved the kids, all five of
them. Everything about her was right.

Joe decided not to waste any more
time. He took her out one evening in the
spring, and when he took her home, they sat
in the car for a while talking. Then Joe took a
deep breath and said,

"Sara, what would you think about
getting married?"
"Is that a proposal?"

"Yes."

"Then, I think I would like that."

"Is that a 'yes"?

"Yes."

"How does July sound to you?"

"That sounds good to me."

So on July 12, 1970, less than seven months after they met, Sara married Joe in a ceremony in a Methodist Church in Batesburg. Jerry Wessinger was Joe's best man, and Robert was able to be there, too.

Sara moved into Joe's house on Live Oak Road. She already loved Robert, and she knew she would love all of Joe's children as though they were her own. Both Sara and Joe wanted to make sure Joe's children had a happy home whenever they could come.

Because of the divorce, Joe had to leave the Catholic church, and since Sara was a Methodist, they decided to attend Bethany United Methodist Church in Summerville.

Service was held in a beautiful chapel called Spell chapel. Joe liked the church, and he enjoyed the adult Sunday School class that he and Sara attended together.

One Sunday night, shortly after they were married, they were coming back from the Edisto River around 2:00 or 3:00 am. Joe's new bride, said, "I would really love a watermelon. Joe, please get me one."

John Wessinger was driving the car, and they could see the light of a full moon shining on a watermelon field. Joe ordered John, "Stop the car."

Joe and Sara got out and crawled under the barbed wire fence to get to the watermelon. When he picked one out, Sara said, "Not that one." Joe pointed to another one, and she said, "No, find a bigger one."

Joe couldn't help but think about how earlier that summer, in July, while on Air Force maneuvers, a farmer shot a guy stealing apples. Now his wife was in someone else's watermelon patch looking for a bigger watermelon.

They continued up the hill before Sara found one she liked. The following Sunday, Joe told the story of stealing the watermelon to the class and joked about Sara making him risk their lives to find the biggest one.

Sara didn't say anything. When they got in the car to drive home, she finally spoke, "I'm never going back to that Sunday School class."

Sara and Joe settled into happily married life. On the weekends, they enjoyed time with the Wessingers, and when Joe had to go to McEntire Joint National Guard Base, they would ride up together.

Sara would drop him off, go visit her family, pick him up on Sunday, and then drive home together. They were happy, but Joe's children were always on their minds.

It was around this time that Robert, 12, woke up one night on the floor of his step-father's ex-wife's home in Nebraska. Again, he didn't know where his mother was or where he would be the next night.

He got up and found the phone and dialed his father collect. Joe answered the ring and heard Robert's voice, " Dad, can you please send me money to come home?"

Joe went to Western Union and wired him the money for airfare, and Robert flew home. He had made his final decision.

Robert was relieved to come home to his steady, reliable father and his stable and welcoming stepmother. He quickly adjusted to life with his father and Sara and to living without his mother or brother or sisters.

Joe and Sara took him to church with them, and after the early service, they attended Sunday school. Robert became part of the Methodist Youth Fellowship (MYF) and made good friends.

He was glad to be in his own house and sleep in his own room. He was glad to go back to school in Summerville where he liked his teachers and had always excelled.

He was in the seventh grade, but none of his records had transferred. He spent the next three years working hard to get placed back into the advanced classes he should have been in all along.

Robert began to realize that his father had been tough on them for a reason. Joe was trying to teach them the important lesson that opportunity is found through hard work, and that it takes hard work and sacrifice to provide a good home.

Robert learned that the reason Joe and Sara were able to provide them with the security of a good home was because they had developed the discipline and responsibility required of an adult to take care of the necessities of life.

Robert's clothes might not always have been the right size for him, and he might have gone sometimes without a haircut before Sara came into their lives, but he knew he was always secure with his father and stepmother.

Robert learned from his father's example. Joe demonstrated everyday how to become a responsible, trustworthy, hardworking and successful person. However, Robert didn't get the benefit of learning from his father about how to talk to girls!

When Robert turned 13, Joe and Sara threw him a birthday party, and Robert was excited. He wanted to be sure Linda, a girl he had his eye on, came to his party. His plan was to go see the movie, "The Yellow Submarine," and sit by Linda.

The day came, and Robert's buddies showed up, and so did Linda. Robert totally ignored her, and she stayed close to his sisters and ignored him. But the party was a big success, and Robert was happy to belong in this loving, happy family with Joe and Sara.

Robert admired the band program at school and decided that he really wanted to learn to play the trumpet and join the band. Joe got a rental instrument for him so he could try it out.

Every day Robert stayed up in his room and practiced for two hours. Sara and Joe never complained, and eventually Robert learned how to play well.

Being in the band became the most formative experiences in school for Robert, and Joe could see how Robert's confidence grew and how happy it made him to be in the band.

When Robert got really good on the trumpet, he told his father he needed a better one. Joe told him to play for him so he could see for himself how good Robert was.

Robert played, and Joe said, "That's good, son. We'll go ahead and order it," and, to Robert's surprise and pleasure, he ordered one of the finest trumpets made from Fox Music in Charleston.

Robert didn't know how his dad had come up with money. When it arrived, Fox called Joe, "The horn you ordered is here." Joe said, "We'll be there to pick it up soon."

When they got there, Joe took out his wallet, expecting to pay maybe up to $100 for it. They said, "Your total is $650." Joe was shocked, but he tried to hide it from Robert.

Robert was more motivated than ever to practice, and he got to be so good at playing the trumpet that he earned first chair in the renowned Summerville High School Band under the excellent direction of the talented and beloved Gus Moody.

Of all the children, Robert was the only one who stayed with Joe constantly from the time he was twelve until he was grown and on his own. Robert states it has made all the difference in his life.

He went to church with Joe, helped him in his business, and did whatever his father asked him to do. When Robert was a child, Joe put him to work cleaning the shop, and now that Joe worked as a home builder, he rode his bike to job sites to clean them.

For a couple of years, Robert was the only child who lived with Joe and Sara. Then, in 1973, Joe and Sara were blessed by the birth of their baby girl, Beth.

Joe wished all of his children could be together under his roof. Kathy and Lola came when they could, but they weren't able to come often until they were on their own. Eventually, Kathy finished school and got married, and she and her husband, Terry, came to live near Joe.

Then Paul said he was coming home, too. He stayed for a while until he got mad at his father again and returned to his mother living then in Florida. After six months, Paul came home again, and this time, he stayed until he finished school.

Lola, the last to rejoin the fold, finished school in Florida and finally was able to return to her childhood home, reunite with her father and siblings, and become part of the family again.

Sara made home a welcoming place for all the children when they came to visit and when they moved back home to stay.

She cooked regular meals for Joe and the children, and she made sure that the family sat down to them together.

They all went to church together where Sara proudly introduced them as her children. Sara's peaceful, sweet nature made home a safe and nurturing place. Soon, they started calling her Mom, and she loved them and treated them like they were her own.

She and Joe also made sure they had fun as a family. One of their favorite outings was going to Short Stay. Because Joe was a veteran, he was able to take the family to this recreational area on the lake reserved for the military.

By now Joe could afford a boat, so he took them out on Lake Moultrie at Short Stay almost every weekend, and everyone, including Kathy and Terry, would load up in the boat to water ski and go tubing.

After spending all day on the water, they came in tired, happy, and sunburned, and Joe grilled hamburgers. For some reason, the hamburgers tasted extra good after they had been on the water all day.

One time, Paul was driving the boat and pulling Joe on skis. Suddenly, Joe clipped something in the water and fell. Paul circled back around to throw him the rope.

Suddenly an alligator broke the surface of the water with its mouth gaping wide. Joe spit out water, grabbed the rope, and, nearly standing on his skis, shouted, "Go, dummy, go, go, go!!!!"

Life was good, and Joe's walk with the Lord had grown closer and closer. He had begun the habit of waking up early every morning and to begin his day with Bible reading and prayer.

The Lord had heard the prayers Joe had cried out for his children during those hard years apart and had restored them to him under his roof or close by. His prayers for a faithful, loving wife had been answered, and he had Sara by his side.

Joe thanked God for his blessings and for giving him another chance to have a good marriage, a happy home, and a close family. And he continued to pray for the loved ones he had left behind in Lithuania.

Joe and Sara

Joe, Sara, Robert, Paul, Beth

Chapter 12

The Road to Success

"The Lord was with Joseph, so he became a successful man. And the Lord was with him, and he was a prosperous man in all things; and he dwelt in his master's house." (Genesis 39:2)

Joe had been working on the Charleston Air Force Base as a civil engineer in the cabinet shop for a couple of years when he heard they had an opening for a civil engineer officer.

The pay looked great, but the applicant had to have an Associate Degree in Engineering. Joe wanted that job, so he decided it was time for him to finish his education. He began what would become a twelve-year journey to success.

Joe's determination to get his degree and the job impressed his superiors. In 1960, they decided to promote him to Civil Engineering Officer with the requirement that he would continue to make progress on earning his degree.

Joe was true to his word, and he never stopped pursuing his degree until he achieved it. He tried to enroll at Trident Tech, but the admissions officer told him that he needed to get a US high school diploma first.

So Joe enrolled in adult education night classes at Summerville High School where he became good friends with the principal, Olin McCurry, who also attended Joe's church.

(Years later, Olin's wife, Rose, taught Robert calculus, and Olin's daughters, Rosie and Laura, became his good friends. The three teens knew each other through their church youth group, and Rosie was his classmate at school.

Laura's first job was teaching physics at Summerville High School where Robert, a national science fair award winner, became her star student. He understood much more about Physics than Laura did, but he never flaunted his superior knowledge.

Instead, he came in to set up labs for her before school and during his lunch break, and he volunteered to solve difficult problems on the chalk board. On several occasions, Laura

*understood the solutions that eluded her by
following Robert's board work.*)

When Joe finished his GED from
Summerville, he still needed to work on his
English skills, so he enrolled in English
classes at The Baptist College, now
Charleston Southern University.

There he became friends with another
immigrant, George Niketas, the head of the
English department. In two years, Joe was
ready for the program at Trident Tech where
he studied until he earned an associate
degree in Civil Engineering in 1971.

With his hard-earned degree in hand,
Joe made GS-9, (the 9th pay grade in the
General Schedule pay scale, for employees
in mid-level positions in the Civil Service).

Joe's responsibilities included paving
airfields and maintaining family housing,
taxiways, and runways. Joe inspected a
house whenever someone moved out and
made any necessary repairs for the 900
housing units.

When Joe made inspections and
repairs, he had to make estimates and get
the materials. He had to compile local
weekly and monthly reports, and he had to

go to Air Force command every quarter to report on the status of projects.

On top of all of that, Joe was responsible for accounting for non-appropriated funds, like funds for the library, chapel, and clubs.

One day Joe was at work in the shop making a cutting board when he got the idea that it would be nice to put some handles in the wood. It would be easy enough to just cut them out.

Joe got a ¾ round over knife, but it wasn't cutting deep enough. Joe looked around and saw another man in the shop working with the table saw, so he asked him to help him cut the handles by holding the board on top of the table saw while Joe cut.

The saw wasn't cutting into the board right, so the man cranked it up faster. This didn't solve the problem because the blade wasn't tall enough.

Then it all happened in an instant. Joe's hand dropped under the saw and blood spurted everywhere. Joe's horrified coworker grabbed some rags nearby and applied pressure to stop the bleeding and rushed Joe to the hospital.

Doctors worked to save Joe's fingers, but the tips were gone, and there was nothing they could do. Joe lost several fingers down to the first knuckle.

Always conscientious, in only three days with his fingers still bandaged and healing, Joe was back at work, and gradually, he got used to working that way.

He was thankful for the work and the significant raise, but he was increasingly unhappy about working with men who had a variety of problems that affected their work, particularly drinking.

Joe's boss couldn't wait for happy hour, and he began it at lunch. Joe's boss frequently got drunk and became increasingly unreliable.

However, the Chief Engineer, a full Colonel and a graduate of MIT, was on the ball and strictly business. Colonel Hanna liked Joe and started calling on Joe to check on any reported problems and did what he could to support Joe.

One time when his boss was away on leave, a project came up that his boss had estimated would cost $137,000. However, he had left out the ceiling, refrigeration, paneling on the wall, etc., and the cost came closer to $200,000.

Joe was responsible for coming up with a solution quick. The Chief Engineer knew Joe wouldn't have made a $63,000 mistake, so he stepped in to work with Joe to get it straightened out.

The Colonel reprimanded Joe's boss when he returned from leave. Joe's boss thought Joe was trying to get his job. He confronted Joe, and Joe assured him he wasn't even qualified for the boss's job and had no intention of trying to get it.

Nonetheless, the disagreements began and continued one after another, and working with his boss became even more unpleasant.

Joe was also sick of working with the other guys who spent all their time at work drinking, gambling, and playing cards and talking about women and television shows.

When Colonel Hanna retired, Joe decided it was time for him to leave, too. He had 1200 hours sick leave coming to him, but he decided to just walk away and leave all those hours behind along with the people he couldn't stand working with anymore.

Throughout all of these years, Joe supplemented his income by spending his weekends building furniture and cabinets for friends, first out of the small workshop that he built at his home on Butler street and then out of his garage on Live Oak Road.

So in 1972, he quit his job, talked Dwayne McCubbin into starting a business with him, took out his $18,000 retirement, leased a building built by his friend Jack Salisbury at 606 North Gum Street, and started Custom Woodcraft, a cabinet shop.

For the first eight months, people he trusted wouldn't pay him after he had done the work, and money for jobs didn't come in. Joe worried that he might have made the wrong decision and would lose it all.

One of those jobs was to remodel 26 townhomes in Charleston. But there was a problem. Joe was following what the group of architects laid out for him to do, but when Joe read the building codes, he read that houses couldn't be higher than 27 feet.

The plans called for building the garages underneath the houses, but during every high tide, the water would rise right up through the ground into the house up to 26 inches high into the garage, and then drain away again during low tide.

Joe called the issue to the attention of the architects, but they said, "There's nothing to worry about, Joe, and, anyway, it's not your problem." All Joe could do was say, "I guess you're right."

So he worked hard to elevate two houses, tore down some, and started to work on building the others. When he had finished one house, they landscaped the yard and held an open house.

During the open house, a storm came up--and so did the water. It came up so high that women had to pull up their skirts when they walked out. The recently planted bushes were floating down the street.

Joe kept making the renovations although he hadn't received payment yet. Then workmen arrived and prepared to add pools.

The day before they blew in the concrete for the pools, Joe approached the main engineer who scowled and asked,

"What's your problem now."

Joe said, "I want you to consider if the pool is in too low. To elevate those houses and put in the garages, they took out 26 inches of dirt."

The engineer replied, "Are you an engineer?"
"No I'm not."
"Well, I am."

They finished the pool. The tide came in, and shrimp swam in the pool. To correct the problem, workmen put in storm drains.

Joe asked, "Have you ever dealt with storm drains?"
"No."
"They're difficult to take care of."
"Joe, it's not your concern."

Later, manholes over the drains rattled with the water rising beneath them.

The engineer accused Joe of not following the specifications to make them watertight, but when he checked, he found out that Joe Had done them exactly right.

By Thanksgiving, they owed Joe $384,600 for the work he had done. They called Joe into the office. Their lawyer said,

> "Joe, we have good news and bad news. The good news is you can keep working. The bad news is we are bankrupt."

> Joe asked, "How can I work if I don't get money?"

> "You'll get it, Joe," the lawyer promised.

Joe worked another week, and then he decided he couldn't keep working without pay. So he quit and got his own lawyer who was able to help Joe collect $60,000 of the $384,600 they owed him.

At the same time that Joe decided to walk away from the bad situation with the townhouses, he got a job working on a project at Westwood Shopping Plaza on Highway 61.

It was over a million dollar project, and when it was finished, they paid Joe $320,000 more than he expected, which made up for his recent loss.

Joe was thankful that God restored even more than he had lost. God continued to provide Joe with one job after another. Every time Joe thought he was coming close to losing his business and everything else, God threw him a lifeline of new work.

One of these jobs was with Don Haas who asked Joe to build him a finished room over his garage and paid him well for his work. Then Joe got another job like that one, and then another and another.

Before he knew it, he was building houses, and by 1976, he formed Joseph Stasiukaitis Contractor, Inc, Residential and Commercial in Summerville, South Carolina, and Joe had as much work as he could keep up with.

Joe was now a full-time home builder. He built a home and dental office for the Muscotts, a home for the Baileys, the Keifers, Dr. Duncan, a cardiologist, and many other Summerville homes in Ashborough, Ashborough East, and the Tea Farm.

But as with everything else in his life, business wasn't always easy. One of the ongoing problems Joe had to contend with was theft. When Joe was working on condos, thieves constantly stole his materials.

Robert was able to get information about one of the thefts and took the information to the police. The police came up with a ruse to catch the thieves.

They disguised Robert as a buyer looking for 360 rolls of steel and set up the "buy" as a sting operation. Robert wore a wire and sat in a beat-up truck on East Bay Street in a deserted section with $5000 in cash.

Robert waited for the thieves to show up and reminded himself to keep cool and continue acting the part when the police swooped in and pretended to arrest him as they arrested the thieves.

As soon as the thief took the cash for the 360 rolls of roofing steel that he had stolen from Joe's work site, a police car came in siren blaring, followed within 30 seconds by 15 more police cars.

Policemen swarmed the scene with guns drawn. A policeman grabbed Robert and roughly shoved him against a chain link fence. Robert thought in alarm, "This guy stumbled in on the scene and doesn't know I'm part of the sting."

Robert twisted and put his mouth as close as he could to the officer and whispered, "Take it easy. I'm one of you guys!" Robert played his part convincingly, the thieves were busted, and Joe got his steel back.

Another time Joe found himself working with a lot of subcontractors who *all* turned out to be what Joe called "con artists." One of the "con artists" didn't finish the job after he poured the concrete and let the concrete get hard.

He came in with a buddy and demanded, "You've got to pay me now." Joe refused and said, "I'll pay you when you finish the job."

The man and his buddy walked off. Then he came back with a gun and aimed it at Joe. Terrified, Robert called the police. The man left Joe and put his gun in a truck, but before the police arrived, he came back.

This time he had a rifle and threatened Joe again. Joe, without any sign of fear, stubbornly said, "I can't give you the money unless you finish the job."

Before the man could shoot Joe, the police arrived and took both him and his buddy to jail. Joe said he wasn't afraid because he knew they were bluffing.

But when the police checked their guns, they discovered that both of them were loaded. The policeman, Officer Parker, asked Joe, "Do you want to come to the station to press charges?"

Joe surprised him by replying, "No, I don't have grudges. Just take their guns and fine them and let them go." He never heard from them again, and Officer Parker is now an attorney.

Every Friday ended with workers demanding more money for the work they had not finished, not done, or had done poorly. Joe simply shrugged, looked up at them, and said, "If I pay you today, you won't finish the job."

Robert dreaded Fridays and the inevitable arguing with subcontractors. He blamed Joe for trying to hire the cheapest guys he could get who lived hand-to-mouth.

He tried to reason with Joe: "Dad, if you hire reputable people, this wouldn't happen."

Robert recalls one summer when Joe left Robert in charge. Joe warned Robert, "Look out for Randolph Cook, the brick mason. He has not finished his job. Don't you pay him until he has finished the job."

Robert had a pit in his stomach all day on Friday waiting for Randolph, a big strong man with hands like a bear, to come in.

When Randolph came up to Robert that afternoon demanding his pay, Robert didn't look at him and struggled to stammer out, "My dad says I can't pay you until you finish the job."

Randolph leaned his bulk over Robert and growled, "You gonna pay me my damn money now." Robert muttered, "Okay."

Then he spent the rest of the weekend in fear of what Joe would do when he found out. Randolph finished the job, and Joe and Randolph are still friends.

On one occasion, an elderly man poured a concrete driveway that didn't turn out well, and when he came asking for his pay, Joe told him he wasn't about to pay him for the bad work.

The elderly man walked away and opened the door to his pickup truck. Then he showed back up with a rifle that he stuck into Joe's belly and said,

"You *will* pay me, now."

Joe ordered, "Robert, call 911."

The worker shouted, "I will shoot you."

Joe shouted back, "Well then, you'll just have to shoot me."

Just then, the police arrived, disarmed the man, and arrested him. The gun was loaded. Once again, Joe didn't press charges, so the police had to let the man go.

Sometimes these confrontations didn't turn out as well. Robert will never forget one such incident. Joe argued with a subcontractor about the work he had done, and they drove over to work site to look over the man's work.

Once they got there, the subcontractor, over twice as big as Joe, grew even more furious and picked up a 2x4 and smacked Joe in the ribs.

Then he threw the truck keys in the woods and pulled out a post trying to make the entire house fall. Joe was hurt pretty badly. This time, he pressed charges and accused the subcontractor of assault and battery.

Another contractor who had laid ceramic tile demanded his money.

"Did you finish the work?"

"No."

"Then I can't pay you."

Then the tiler pulled a gun and repeated his demand. Jim, Joe's son-in-law, was there and talked to him and managed to get the gun. When the tiler calmed down, Jim gave the gun back to him, and the tiler left.

But not for long. He came back with his gun. This time, when the police came, he fled, and Joe put out an arrest warrant.

Twenty years later, the tiler showed up in Summerville again looking for a job. He was still wanted for assault and battery. Joe decided not to say anything, and the gun-wielding tiler got a government job working for the town.

Paul had this to say about his father's heedless refusal to back down:

> "He is fearless. He has stood up to massive men and poked his chin out and stood his ground.

> Someone threatens to shoot him, and he says, 'Well, you're going to have to shoot me.' Maybe it has something to do with his past.

> In the past, he might have stood up to intimidation just because he was stubborn. But now, it might just be because he has made his peace—he can go any time.

> He just thinks, 'It will be okay--it will be my time. What are you going to do to me? I'm taken care of for eternity.' "

Even when Joe built his own house in the desirable Ashborough subdivision, he ran into what he and Robert had come to think of as the typical problems.

After Joe finished the wiring on his house, John Wessinger said,

> "Joe, something's wrong. We've burned up three coffee pots, and the skill saw is running so fast it sounds like a high-pitched racing motor. It's the best skill saw ever!"

When the power company came out to check on the wiring, they discovered that Joe had wired something at 220 volts instead of 110 volts.

One day after they got the wiring sorted out, a man walked up to the site and started boldly taking the light fixtures, explaining, "I'm the owner." That didn't end well for him.

Joe also sometimes had a problem with plumbing. At one point, when they flushed the toilet, steam came up. But Joe kept working hard, and his beautiful home was built, and his business grew.

Meanwhile, Robert was majoring in Physics at UNC. In his sophomore year, he met cute, dark-haired Brenda Hodge, who was studying Physical Therapy at ECU. By the second date, he was in love, and he knew she was the one.

He was also studying harder than he ever had in his life doing all he could to master the subject, and even though he was one of a handful of successful students in the Physics major, he wasn't really sure how much further he wanted to go with it.

He was hired by MacDonald Douglas to do work on NASA projects while he was still in school and even taught classes, but more than anything, he wanted to get married to Brenda.

NASA offered him a job in California, but he didn't want to go out there, and he particularly didn't want to leave Brenda who was finishing her degree.

Joe's business was growing, and he was doing well. By the time Robert graduated in 1981, Joe could offer Robert a full-time job. Robert decided that the fastest route to marrying Brenda was to start working for his dad.

Robert's first independent assignment was to build a home in Rock Hill,

South Carolina. As soon as he finished the house, he and Brenda got married.

Joe and Robert decided that they should take the South Carolina General Contractors License test. They passed it, and Joe got a license to start JRS Builders, Inc., a commercial and residential construction company, on Trolley Road in Summerville.

Robert worked with Joe for the next nine years. The business continued to be a success, but for Robert and Brenda, it was a painful success.

Robert still dreaded every Friday afternoon when there were the usual arguments with Joe complaining about unfinished or poor work and the workers demanding their pay.

Joe, who was never an orthodox bookkeeper, managed the books, and this frustrated Robert, too. When customers asked for changes or additions to the job, Joe agreed to do the work.

The problem was that he wouldn't add up the cost until he finished the project, and the customers were often shocked as some estimates came in up to $20,000 over the initial estimate.

Robert also found it hard to watch his dad, a serious Christian, yell at his workers every Friday. But what disturbed Robert most of all was that, although he and Joe were partners, Joe was still making all of the decisions.

Robert worked all the time, and Brenda wanted him to have more time to enjoy spending with her and their two small sons. Robert decided that it was time to go out on his own.

He had spent nine long years without a real vacation and no days off from the responsibilities. He had worked with unreliable, dishonest people, and he had learned from watching, helping, and working alongside Joe for all these years.

Brenda, who had a stable income as a physical therapist, would do whatever she could to support him in his decision.

He could control whom he hired, and he would hire honest people whom he wouldn't have to always watch to keep them from stealing from him.

They wouldn't be subcontractors; they would be his employees. He could focus on cabinet work and become the best in the area.

The only problem was getting a loan, and Joe, who was still teaching Robert life lessons, came through with a loan for Robert at 12% interest, and he also had a shop and tools that Robert could rent so he could start his business, Lowcountry Case and Millwork.

Robert hired his brother, Paul, and his brother-in-law, Terry Hensley, and in 1990, Lowcountry Case and Millwork was open for business.

By 2000, Joe owned Corey Gardens Townhouse and three commercial properties in Summerville, and he was ready to start slowly scaling back JRS Builders.

At the same time, Lowcountry Case and Millwork was ready to expand, so Joe designed and ordered the plans from an architect and built a big office and customized the facility in Ladson based on what Robert wanted.

At the new facility, Joe came in more and more to do personal projects for himself and others. Over the course of several months, Joe started to help with Lowcountry Case and Millwork projects.

Finally, one day Joe came in to the office and walked up to Robert and said, "You're going to have to hire me, but you'll have to pay me!"

After decades of being his own boss, Joe had a hard time adjusting to being an employee again. Robert set up a corner of the shop just for Joe so he could do custom work.

He described his dad's fierce independence: "You can't control him; you can only hope to contain him!"

What Joe, the young, uneducated, Lithuanian immigrant, started in his garage continued to increase in success for 25 years. His business became well known for its high-standard, quality work.

Their reputation extended throughout the tri-county area and to other areas of the state like Rock Hill, Hilton head, Seabrook Island, Kiawah Island, and even to an island where Joe put in custom-made cabinets for the Air Base Commander.

He experienced the satisfaction and pride of watching his son's business, Lowcountry Case and Millwork (LCCM), thrive and win awards. The next generation had taken what he started from nothing and had grown and succeeded beyond his dreams.

(15 years later, Robert passed the reins to his son, David, and Joe proudly watched David build a new state-of-the-art facility and triple the size of LCCM.)

Lowcountry Case and Millwork, 2018
Ribbon-cutting ceremony for new
52,000-square-foot facility

Robert, Brenda, Joe, Mayor Keith Sumney
David (Joe's grandson and president of
LCCM), and Amy, David's wife

Part Four:
The Lord Calls

174

Chapter 13

The Calling

"For we are his workmanship, created in Christ Jesus for good works, which God prepared beforehand, that we should walk in them." (Ephesians 2:10)

Going to church and attending mass were as essential to Joe's upbringing as doing his chores or gathering around the table for meals.

From the time he was a small child, he had taken his turn with his brothers, put on the clothes reserved for Sunday, and walked proudly with his father to the cathedral over three miles away.

He had watched as his mother put aside food for his father to take to church for the Stasiukaitis family's contribution to the priest's salary.

He had waited every Christmas for the priest's visit to their home to collect the food they had saved for him just as the rest of the impoverished parishioners had done.

He had been glad and proud that his family had been able to make their contribution to God's servant who would have had no food to eat without their sacrificial giving.

During his terrifying exodus through unrelenting bombing and treacherous, mine-filled fields, and during the forced deportations in cold, crowded boxcars to unknown destinations, Joe prayed for his life, and he had a sense of God's protection.

When he was a refugee and grieved over never seeing his family again, the priest was a comforting presence in the camps who encouraged Joe and the other displaced flocks.

Joe spent the rest of his youth after the war in a Catholic orphanage where he continued the familiar rites of worship he had known as a child. There, a priest visited regularly, so Joe was able to study his catechism and receive his first communion.

When Joe immigrated to the United States, he was surprised and relieved to find a Lithuanian Catholic church in the Bronx, and when he moved on to Scranton, he sought out another Catholic church.

He faithfully attended both churches, but despite his dedication, Joe didn't consider himself to be much of a Christian. He was a Stasiukaitis, and Stasiukaitis's were Catholic and attended church.

After he joined the Air Force, he became friends with non-Catholic Christians, and as he started to get to know them, he sometimes would go to church with them.

He noticed a difference in the way they practiced their faith, and he began to want to learn more about what it meant to be a Christian.

Joe had heard about God all of his life, and he was thankful that he had been protected and spared during the war, but he began to realize that he didn't really know much about God.

Although he had called out to God to protect him during his ordeals, he had simply repeated the prayers he had been taught, and he didn't know how to pray to Him or follow Him in the personal way he saw other Christians do.

In 1956, convinced that a proper marriage must be presided over by a Catholic priest, his wedding was a Catholic ceremony. When children came, he took them to church just as faithfully as Tomas had taken him.

Then, when his marriage started to fall apart, he went to the priest for counseling, and he was told that if he divorced, he could no longer receive Holy Communion.

During this time of heartache and turmoil, Joe grew uncertain about what he truly believed. He was a churchgoer, and he knew you had better know God to have eternal life, but he wasn't sure that he knew God.

He even questioned the fairness of God. Why was Joe going to be denied communion when he was not the one responsible for ruining his marriage? For the first time, he started looking for answers in the Bible himself.

He remained a loyal parishioner at St. John's Catholic Church, attending mass every Sunday, contributing his carpentry skills on weekends and after work, and serving as president of the Catholic Men's Club at their request. But the priest remained immovable.

Then he met and married Sara, a dedicated Christian Methodist, and because Joe wanted to receive Holy Communion, he made the decision to leave the Catholic church.

He would try a Methodist church, which had an open communion table, where he, Sara, and Robert could worship together, and his other children could join them, too, when they were home.

In 1970, they started attending Bethany United Methodist Church in Summerville. The minister, Red Williams, came to visit Joe, and Joe was impressed by the depth of Red's confident, strong, and down-to-earth faith.

He looked forward to hearing Red's sermons, and he and Sara joined a Sunday school class where they made good friends. Day by day, his faith deepened, and he felt a growing desire to draw closer to the Lord and to know Him more personally.

Then Joe and Sara made the decision to join the church. For Sara, it was a transfer of membership; for Joe, it was a profession of a new-found faith and an even deeper commitment.

As the 70's passed, Joe's life became one of stability and blessing. In Sara, he had found the wonderful, loving wife he had prayed for, and his children had gained a mother who welcomed them with eager, open arms.

His business was booming beyond his dreams, so much so, that his friends tell a story about a crazy moment of celebration in Las Vegas when Joe lit a cigar with a $100 bill.

But it wasn't Joe's nature to be a flagrant spender, and as he looked at his life, his wife, his children, and his success, he was overwhelmed by how good God had been to him, and he felt the urge to give back.

He had always had a heart for children, and even when he was still getting on his feet, he had volunteered to do the ongoing repairs for the Jenkins Orphanage in Charleston.

He felt compelled to show his love to God and to be a good steward, but what did the Lord want him to do with all that he had been given? He began to look for more opportunities to bless those in need around him.

One day after publicizing an urgent need, a Salvation Army worker looked up from his prayers as another dirty, weary, poor soul approached him in need of help. It was Joe. He had come straight from work to drop off a check.

In fact, because Joe gave 50% of his profits away to worthy causes, the IRS audited him. He was able to produce every receipt and account for every penny.

Joe threw himself into serving Bethany as he had served St. Johns. When the church needed renovations, Joe formed a team of volunteers.

He began what was to become lifelong practice of donating his nonwork time and skills to Bethany and his material wealth wherever and whenever they were needed.

Joe's minister, Red Williams, was appointed to another church. He was followed by other great ministers, and Joe became a loyal server and friend of each one.

With Joe's increasing commitment to service and fellowship and under the leadership of ministers like Reverends James Alewine, Harold Lewis, and Needham Williamson, his faith put down deep roots and grew strong.

Joe often found himself teamed up with Marion Dorn, who, like Joe, shared his faith through acts of service. They took on cooking steak dinners for the men's club together.

Once someone asked, "Can we have something besides steak?" Joe's quick and definite answer was, "No." Later, he relented, and he and Marion added oyster stew to the menu.

One time, they were talking and drinking a little wine while they were making the stew, and somehow mushrooms they had chopped for the salad got added to the stew.

When some men commented, "We've never had mushrooms in our stew before," Joe, without missing a beat, matter-of-factly informed them, "It's a new recipe."

These two quiet, dedicated servants of the Lord made a good team. They prayed together and served together. If something needed to be done, Joe and Marion could be found hard at work together, making sure that it got done.

At the end of the seventies, Harold Lewis, who, at 44, was Joe's age, came to serve as Bethany's new minister. Joe's large adult Sunday school class gave Harold a welcoming party.

Although Joe was not particularly outgoing, in his quiet manner, he let Harold know that he was pleased Harold had come, and he made sure that Harold felt very welcome.

Harold sensed from the first that here was a Christian man he would be able to count on, someone who would be there for him and the church, and someone who would let anyone know where he stood.

And Harold was right; Joe was always there, and at any significant gathering, he would see Joe with Sara and their little girl, Beth.

At that time, the church's 2000 members were bursting out of Spell Chapel. James Alewine, now the district superintendent, advised Harold, "If you come down here, you're going to have to figure out a way to build a new sanctuary."

Harold didn't have to wonder long where he would find help. Joe stepped up and in his behind-the-scenes way, he started working to make sure Bethany had a new sanctuary.

Joe and Harold worked together for years on this project, laughing and sometimes crying together. Harold would often find Joe at work, and just as often, he heard him exclaim in his strong Lithuanian accent, "I'm so aggrawated!"

Joe might have been aggravated, but he was undaunted. When Harold got discouraged, Joe would say, "We'll get through this. We'll make it work." And they did.

Harold recalls,

"Joe was involved in the life and support of Bethany in all the ways written in the Methodist Book of Discipline.

When Joe joined the church, he promised to 'faithfully participate in its ministries by his prayers, his presence, his gifts, and his witness.' And he kept his promises.

Joe wasn't someone who went around putting on a pious face, but he was generous with his presence and his gifts, and he was always in the forefront of contributing to whatever cause the church was sponsoring."

Joe's servant discipleship, his presence at church, and his care for the shepherd of the flock demonstrated to anyone who knew him the value he placed on supporting what he believed in.

Joe felt it was his responsibility to do what he could to take care of the preachers, and he took it upon himself to treat them to the good food Charleston had to offer.

He and Sara took Harold and his wife, Edna, out at least twice a month, picking them up in his big Lincoln Continental and chauffeuring them to Charleston as though Harold was a celebrity.

Joe insisted that they order everything a gourmand could appreciate. This included escargot, Joe's favorite, and rack of lamb, which Harold recalled was the last meal they ordered together before Harold's appointment at Bethany ended.

Joe was a big fan of the University of North Carolina (UNC) since Robert had earned his degree in physics from there. In 1983, Joe's team was ranked 5th in the nation, and he planned to go see them take on the University of South Carolina (USC).

USC had never been able to beat UNC in years of rivalry. Since Harold had played football for the USC, Joe invited him to travel with him to watch the big game.

On the five hour ride up, they stopped at a western wear shop, and Harold set his eyes on a rodeo cowboy hat. He picked it up, and he saw that it was the hottest thing going. He had to have it.

Wearing his new hat, he went into the stadium with Joe. In a great upset, USC beat UNC, badly. It was a thrill for Harold, but it was a quiet ride home. Harold was never invited to go with Joe to a game again, but he kept the hat.

Although Harold never had much of an opportunity to wear it again, he's glad he bought the hat because he looks at it every day, and he thinks of Joe and what Joe has meant to him.

He remembers how Joe helped him in any way he could, and how Joe enabled and empowered him to take on the big task of building a new sanctuary.

Today, Bethany United Methodist Church worships in a beautiful sanctuary that has served the congregation well. Harold adds quietly, with apparent love and respect, "Joe gave that to me, to the church, and to the Lord."

By the 80's, Joe was an established and successful businessman. He was an active and valued member of Bethany and steadily growing in his faith.

He and Sara had created a wonderful home. He was proud of Robert and grateful that he had come home to be with them, and he doted on smart little Beth.

However, all was not well. Joe was troubled by serious concerns about his other children. He regretted that he only saw Kathy and Lola when they visited once or twice a year, and he was particularly worried about Paul.

Paul had finally come home to stay when he was 16. He was smart, a good athlete, and a good student in high school, but during his first year at Spartanburg Methodist College, he got into drugs, and his life turned into a chaotic mess.

Under the influence of drugs, Paul's personality changed, so that Joe and Paul couldn't sit down to a meal together without a blow up. Eventually, Joe couldn't even be in the same room with him.

Then one day, Joe had a call from the police in Richmond, Virginia. Paul was in jail, and he was suicidal. Joe drove to Richmond to get Paul, but on the ride home Paul wouldn't even look at him.

Joe brought Paul home and spent hours on his knees praying that he would go straight. Paul didn't want to stay in the house with Joe, so Joe and Robert helped Paul move into Weathers Apartments nearby in Summerville. Then suddenly, Paul was gone.

Mrs. Weathers was reluctant to let them into Paul's apartment. When they finally got in, they looked around in shock.

Everything was gone, his clothes, the television, and all the furniture. Nothing was left. He had taken everything.

Months went by with no word from Paul, until he finally got in touch. He was in Atlanta where his mother now lived. He said he wanted to come back.

He needed a job, so Joe gave him one. He wanted a car, so Joe got him a brand new Chevy Cavalier. Joe let him live in one of the townhouses he had built.

Paul stayed a few months. Then he was in an accident. As soon as he received his insurance money, he hocked everything, left the car, and left town. He was gone again.

When he finally came back, he informed them that he was getting married. It would be at Hampton Park in Charleston. Joe and Sara went to it, despite their pain that Paul had gone out of his way to make sure it was a secular wedding.

The relationship between Paul and Joe was rockier than ever, and Paul blamed Joe for their problems because Joe had spent his life working all the time. They couldn't see eye-to-eye on anything, and Paul was always angry.

He thought everyone was against him and carried around an enormous chip on his shoulder. He worked in nightclubs, enjoyed the nightlife, and sang and played bass in a blues band, dreaming of becoming a great bass player.

He rebelled against everything Joe believed in, and when Joe held the line and said, "This is how we do things," Paul retorted, "This is how you do things" and did the opposite.

The worry and grief over Paul drove Joe to his knees, and he prayed hard, pouring his heart out to God for him every day. He realized that he was helpless to help Paul, and he knew that only God could rescue his son.

After three years, he prayed one more time,

"Well, Lord, I don't know. I just don't know what to do. I don't know how to help him or how to reach him. I am putting him in your hands."

He gave up on reaching Paul himself and trusted God to save him. Strangely, Joe knew that this surrender brought him even closer to God.

During this time, Joe faced other trials, and sometimes, it seemed like everything was going against him. In addition to his heartache about Paul, his business was giving him headaches.

He couldn't find people who wouldn't steal from him, let alone find decent employees, and he was sick of it. There were problems at Bethany, too.

He loved his preacher and his church, but the members were experiencing the turmoil and upheaval of growing pains, and Joe didn't know what the future held for his church or for him. He spent a lot of time praying.

Then in 1985, Needham Williamson, Bethany's new minister, came to town, and Joe soon discovered that the Lord had something else in mind for this 52 year old, Lithuanian immigrant to do, something that would become his life's true calling.

When Needham began his ministry at Bethany, the recent explosion in size brought excitement and celebrated growth, and it brought inevitable change.

Bethany members were proud of their beautiful new sanctuary, but they grieved for the small intimate church they had been.

In the midst of the upheaval, among those who were uncertain and unsettled, Needham found Joe, a rock-solid, fervent supporter he could count on.

Like the other ministers, Needham quickly developed a deep appreciation and affection for Joe. Whenever the church had a need, Needham could call on Joe.

Joe would take Needham and another member out to dinner to talk things over. Joe would always pay for the meal, and the member would usually commit to help.

Over time, Joe spent thousands of dollars on dinners, and the church completed innumerable projects.

When Ray Litts came to Bethany to be interviewed for the Associate Minister position, Needham said, "There's a guy I want you to meet," and he put in a call to Joe.

They arranged to meet for lunch the next day, and Ray realized that it was understood that Joe was going to "get stuck with the bill."

When Ray was hired, he didn't have to look long for a place to live; Joe set him up to lease one of the townhouses he had built in Corey Woods.

When Joe heard that Ray was interested in woodworking, he invited him to come to his shop, and he set aside a place for Ray to work.

Ray loved working at Joe's shop. He chuckled, "That's where I learned Robert's and Paul's real names: 'dammit Robert' and 'jackass Paul.' "

He also learned that Joe was quick to get annoyed, quick to get over it, and quick to see the humor of a situation.

Ray tells of an incident when an employee made a costly mistake:

"Robert was pretty mad. and he started 'blessing' out the employee.

The more Robert thought about that stupid mistake, the more irritated he got, so he lit into the worker again. To make sure he'd gotten his point across, Robert let him have it a third time.

Joe must have decided it was time to run interference. He stepped up to Robert, grinned up at him, and said, 'I think he understands.' "

Another time, Ray was working on his corner cabinet when Joe said, "I want you to take these three bulletin boards to the church."

Ray was happy to do that, but he noticed there were four bulletin boards. He also noticed that Joe was steamed about something, so he hesitated to point out there were four, not three bulletin boards.

To clarify the assignment, he asked, "These four?" And Joe replied impatiently, "That's what I said!" Confident now, Ray picked up all four bulletin boards, and Joe exclaimed, "I SAID THREE!"

Ray realized that Joe was a great source of wisdom, and he learned to be humble enough to accept Joe's counsel.

When Joe asked Ray if he had gotten something done, Ray would start to explain why he hadn't been able to accomplish the task.

Joe would interrupt him, and say, "I'm not interested in your excuses; I'm just interested in the results. Don't tell me about your labor pains. I just want to see the baby."

The feisty Lithuanian had another expression he would mutter from time to time: "Some people complain if you hang them with a new rope."

The best source of wisdom was the tradition Joe started that has lasted through decades of friendship. Joe always closed a conversation with, "Let's end with a little prayer." Then he prayed for Ray, as he has continued to do every day.

One day, Needham came to Joe to talk with him about the sad situation of Dr. Harold Elliott, an elderly Methodist medical missionary. Dr. Elliot had devoted much of his life to helping people in need.

Beginning in 1938 in the mountains of Kentucky, Dr. Elliott rode on horseback to reach his patients, and then traveled on to Nigeria where he worked to fulfill his calling on the mission field until 1953.

Later, he returned to Minnesota to raise a family and established a successful practice. After his wife died, Dr. Elliot returned to the mission field in 1971.

He came to serve the impoverished and isolated community of Johns Island and lived in a used, donated mobile home. He drew on his own funds to set up a clinic.

At the clinic, he charged his patients $1.00 a visit and gave them medicine at his own expense. By 1988, he was living on Social Security in a dilapidated mobile home with a leaking and sagging roof.

Joe went out to meet Dr. Elliot. After assessing his living situation, Joe exclaimed to Needham in dismay, "It's a disgrace for a man who had given so much for the church and others to have to live like that!"

At that time, Joe was building a Thrifty Car Rental building on Montague Avenue in Charleston, and he was going to have to knock down a thirty-year-old six room house on the property.

With some added rooms and extensive renovation, Joe thought he could turn it into a good home for Dr. Elliott.

So Joe took the first step and hired a professional mover to move the old house from the Thrifty Rental property to John's Island where they would repair and renovate it to give to Dr. Elliott.

After watching the movers put the house in place, Joe and Needham returned to the parsonage to talk about their long-term plans for recruiting a team of volunteers to help with all the work necessary to make the house ready.

Bethany was still struggling to get back on its feet and dealing with what was threatening to become chronic in-fighting. Needham had been praying for a solution.

As they stood in the driveway outside of the parsonage with the moon shining bright, Needham turned to Joe and said,

"Joe, let's focus on something besides the church and its problems. Have you ever wanted to go on a mission trip? I've spoken with the United Methodist Volunteers in Mission.

We can send a team on a mission. I'd like to go help the people in Haiti who are suffering and trying to recover from the devastating flooding and hurricanes. Joe, I want you to lead the charge."

That night, Needham and Joe agreed that they would go to Haiti, and Joe would lead the team to build a medical clinic. It was to be the first of many, many mission trips and a pathway for Bethany members to live out the calling of Christ on their lives.

When they returned from Haiti, the work began in earnest on Dr. Elliott's home. Joe enlisted and organized a team of volunteers.

Ray shares the story of how he was recruited:

"Ray," said Joe, "Will you help us on Dr. Elliot's house on Saturday?"

"What time do you want to meet?"

"Early, we'll meet for breakfast."

"Do I need to bring lunch?"

"No, we're only working for half a day."

Early Saturday morning, Ray joined Joe, Robert, and the other volunteers, including a youth team that Robert led. They worked hard throughout the morning.

After noon, Ray started packing up his tools, and Joe walked up, looking surprised:

"Where are you going?"

"You said we're just working half a day."

"That's right. Half a day--7:00 to 7:00."

"Then you'll have to buy me lunch."

So Joe bought him lunch.

Another weekend, Ray arrived before dawn and waited for it to get light as other volunteers gathered at the work site. Joe emerged out of the predawn darkness and strode up to them shouting, "What are you waiting for? You're burning daylight!"

The Bethany Men's club, some of Dr. Elliot's patients, and the youth group worked hard to add a room and bathroom, install central air and heat, paint the building inside and out, and thoroughly renovate and repair it.

When they finished their work, they had turned it into a solid, well-built home, and they decided they should hold a ceremony to dedicate it to Dr. Elliott.

The bishop himself came to give the dedication, and local papers carried the story of the sacrificial service of the missionary and the loving provision of his fellow believers to help him continue to fulfill God's calling to serve the poor.

After the dedication, Joe thought about how much he had enjoyed the whole process. He had built homes and buildings that had cost hundreds of thousands of dollars, but nothing had given him the satisfaction that this work had done.

He had experienced the same depth of peace and satisfaction on the mission trip to Haiti, and he still felt the impact of that trip.

He realized that Bethany had become a place of peace and harmony once again, united in its heart for missions, both at home and abroad. Then it dawned on him: God had given him a new passion, and He had equipped him for a new mission in life.

Joe and team on a local mission

202

Chapter 14

On Mission

"But you will receive power when the Holy Spirit comes upon you. And you will be my witnesses, telling people about me everywhere--in Jerusalem, throughout Judea, in Samaria, and to the ends of the earth." (Acts 1:8 NLT)

As Joe's faith and his gratitude for his blessings deepened, the Lord filled his heart with an even greater desire to serve Him and others. He gave his time and resources at Bethany and supported their mission to help those in need in the community.

He gave between 500-600 hours a year in volunteer hours, and his donations to worthy causes grew to hundreds of thousands of dollars.

The Lord used Joe's hardships to develop a heart of compassion in him for others, and He made Joe aware of the needs of others nearby that particularly touched Joe's heart.

Because he had experienced the insecurity and loneliness of being an orphan, Joe took on the responsibility of keeping the Jenkins Orphanage in good repair.

Because he remembered the trauma of abruptly being pulled from his home and spending years as a displaced youth, he volunteered his skills at Carolina Youth Development Center.

Because he remembered the pain of hunger, in 1984, he was a founding board member of Meals on Wheels, a community program that provides and delivers meals to the homebound, the elderly, and others who are unable to get meals for themselves.

Confident, now, that God had been preparing him all of his life for this new vocation, Joe threw himself into the call with his characteristic energy and zeal.

He accepted the challenge Needham had given to him that night as they stood outside the parsonage. On his first mission trip beyond the Lowcountry, he organized and led 18 Bethany members to Haiti to build a desperately needed eye clinic.

Many of Bethany's most dedicated servant-leaders enthusiastically accepted Joe's invitation to join him and Needham on the inaugural assignment of the Bethany Global Mission team.

18 missioners--including Jackie and Martha Jo Roumillat, Chuck Swenson, Jack Miller, George Keifer, and Tim and Kathy McConnell--became committed members of a growing team, completing scores of missions, near home, in other states, and in other parts of the world.

After a long and tiring day of traveling to Jabo, Haiti, the missioners finally reached their work site located in the middle of a banana field. The conditions were even worse than they had imagined.

The local people barely had enough food to keep from dying of starvation, and they slept in huts with open air toilets that did nothing to help control their chronic susceptibility to life-threatening diseases.

In fact, before the team left the United States, they had been warned about a cholera epidemic sweeping Haiti due to the flooding and terrible sanitation.

Joe sternly warned the others to follow his example and protect themselves, declaring firmly, "I will not touch anybody."

Soon after their arrival, children came running out to greet the missioners, and they surrounded Joe who they quickly learned had brought a lot of candy with him to give to them.

It didn't take long for Joe's resolve to vanish, and he picked up the children and held them in his arms, praying that the Lord would protect him and them, and that everyone would be all right. And they were, and Joe did not get sick.

The team worked hard for the next two weeks, and despite the hardships, the language barrier, and the daily necessity to improvise, they were able to get a lot of work done.

Every night, they gathered together to pray for the Lord's help with the mission and for His provision for the needs of those they came to serve.

Each team member took a turn sharing a devotional. They had contrasting personalities and different work styles, but they were unified in mission and their love for Jesus, and they pulled together to form a remarkably effective team.

Jackie Roumillat and Joe, both builders, sometimes butted heads over what should be done and how they should do it. Jackie, who was more hands-on, was glad to let Joe, the planner and organizer, be the one who directed and pushed the operation.

Jackie would do things the way he liked to do them, and Joe would do things the way he liked to do them, and together, they always got the job done.

One of their many improvisations was making their own bricks. George Keifer and another missionary had put handmade bricks in the sun to harden, but the bricks developed cracks as they dried.

Usually on mission trips, local workers join the team and get paid an hourly wage, and the local Haitian workers began to slop mud on the bricks to keep them from cracking.

They then leveled them and finished them off with the end result of sturdy bricks. George, unaware of the workers' procedure, got in the way of some mud-slopping and got a mouthful of mud.

He yelled out, "Bring me that English-speaking preacher so he can translate what I have to say to this mud-slinger!"

The preacher, who was a full-time missionary and spoke English and Haitian Creole, quickly ran up, assessed the situation, and explained the brick-finishing procedure.

George examined the resulting bricks. Then he asked the missionary to translate, "Keep up the good work," and he returned to laying out the bricks.

On another occasion, Jackie, who was up on a ladder, called out to Martha Jo, Kathy McConnell, and other women volunteers, "Y'all need to come over here and paint the ceiling." They politely declined and informed him: "The ceiling doesn't need it."

Jackie looked from them to the ceiling, and without speaking, got a paint brush, dipped it in blue paint, and flung a large scattered stream of paint up on the ceiling. Then he turned to the astonished women and said evenly, "Now it needs it. Get busy."

The Haitian families lived in grass huts with no modern conveniences like appliances or phones or comforts of any kind. They survived on what their small gardens could produce, mainly yams.

The Haitian yam, a vegetable that looks like a potato but "tastes like a paper napkin," according to Jackie, was the staple of their diet.

Because they had been warned that there would be little food, the mission team brought as much nonperishable food with them as they could carry, particularly canned goods.

The outside porch of the building where they slept looked like a grocery store, lined with all their food and tins. Martha Jo told them that she would make biscuits to go with the canned ham they brought if they could get her some flour.

Motivated, they found some flour and brought it to her, and somehow, she managed to mix the right ingredients together to make biscuits that Joe talks about to this day.

With a grin, Jackie tells a story about their last morning at the mission:

"By the end of the mission, we were down to the very last bit of our food supply. We got up early to eat breakfast for our last meal before we left for the drive to the airport.

A worker came from the kitchen and set down platters of tinned sardines on toast. We passed the platters around the table to all the volunteers.

When they had been passed completely around the table, they witnessed a miracle. The platters were still as full as they had been when they were placed on the table"

Several people who served with Joe on mission trips reported that on more than one occasion, someone would come up and say, "So and so needs something," and Joe would get to work to get the money together and to do whatever it was they needed.

On one particular trip, it had rained that day, and the locals took the missioners up to a place past the church. Everybody was soaking wet by the time they arrived at "a little pitiful frame made of sticks."

The Haitians wanted a roof on the little building and gave Joe all the money they had and asked him if the missioners would put the roof on for them. Joe and the team provided the rest of what was needed from among themselves and built it.

On the mission in Haiti, they all experienced the truth of what the apostle Paul meant when he said in Acts 20:35:

> "In all things I have shown you that by working hard in this way we must help the weak and remember the words of the Lord Jesus, how he himself said, 'It is more blessed to give than to receive.' "

Jackie Roumillat recalls:

> "I get goosebumps when I think about going to Haiti that first time. Needham, our preacher, and my wife Martha Jo went with us, and the plan

for one day was for us to go to church with the locals.

It was something like harvest time or maybe more like Thanksgiving time for them, and their church was way up in the mountains.

It was a good-sized church, but it was crude, with no windows, and as many people outside as inside. They put all of us from the mission team on a sort of platform, like a choir area, and they asked Needham to speak.

Needham spoke, and the missionary who lived there would translate, and when the service started, people were lined up waiting to come into the church to give an offering of whatever they could give.

It was an overwhelming feeling to see those people who had so little bring up whatever they had, even a vegetable. The whole team just sat there crying.

We all wanted to put in something. Joe put in a $100 dollar bill, and then he worried that they wouldn't know what it was, so he told the preacher about it. If Joe had it in his pocket, he would give it."

By the end of two short weeks, they had done what they had come to do and finished the building. They thanked God and prepared for the trip home.

Joe and the team spent the last day giving away things they had brought with them. Joe gave away everything, his shoes, his shirts, and all of his clothes except for his traveling clothes.

He gave all of his money to the mission and workers and their families and had to borrow money from George to buy flip flops to wear on the plane and get lunch at the airport. He only regretted he had not brought more to give away.

After witnessing how the Haitian people gave all they had, Joe decided to travel to Haiti by himself at his own expense the following year to find out what the mission team would need to bring when he returned in 1989.

He brought a team of 14 this time to Jeremi, Haiti. Many of them had come on the first trip, and they had gotten to know the English-speaking, full-time missionary, but they knew he was often called away to serve other villages farther up in the hills.

They were happy to see him there to welcome them back when they arrived. That first night, a rooster must have been glad to see them, too, because he crowed with delight all night long.

On the following night, the rooster was silent to their relief, and they thought that it must have grown accustomed to them. The following evening at supper they were served a meal that included the meat of one chicken.

One of their most special experiences was an expedition that Joe and Jackie went on with the missionary. Jackie recalls:

> "The missionary took us to a tiny church, half the size of our living rooms, with no windows, and we went

inside, and the whole inside and outside of the church was crowded.

I can still feel the vibration in my body of what it felt like in that crowded place when all those people would start singing without an organ or any music. And you hear a completely different sound.

It's the way they sing together. They put their hearts into it. And you could just feel your insides shaking. It was an overwhelming feeling...the presence of God."

Many members of the team were similarly touched by the presence of the Lord among those they came to serve, and they became as passionately committed to the mission work as Joe.

Over the years, Bethany continued to field teams for mission work. Another pastor who came to serve Bethany, Quay Adams, also helped Joe persuade many others to join them, including his sons, Robert and Paul, and one of Bethany's most dynamic and active members, Kevin Dixon.

Kevin was a contractor, too, and skilled in leading. He worked well with Joe and Jackie. Just as Robert caught the passion for missions from Joe, Kevin "caught the bug" from Robert to become one of the team's most influential and dedicated missioners.

Although Robert had served with Joe in local missions for over five years, he couldn't consider going on an overseas mission trip with Joe because someone had to run the business.

But Joe kept urging Robert, "You need to go on a mission trip." Then he promised, "You go on a mission trip, and I'll stay here." Instead of telling Robert where he had to go, he said, " You can choose where you want to go and what you want to do."

In the summer of 1988, with his father's encouragement, Robert went on his first out-of-country mission trip to the Philippines.

Situated near the Taal Vista resort, the mission complex sat on the rim of an extinct volcano. In the morning, missioners had their daily devotion while they sat and looked out over 1000 feet to the rim on the other side of the volcanic caldera.

When they looked down, they saw a vast, stunningly beautiful lake with a mountain rising up from the middle of it and smoke drifting lazily up to the sky.

The chattering of monkeys and the songs of birds provided background music to their prayers and meditation. It was a life-changing experience for Robert as he explained:

> "To spend a week or two with a bunch of people who feel and believe as you do and to do something for people who aren't going to give you anything does something to you.
>
> After a mission trip, I come back with my tank full. It changes my prayers, too. My concerns feel inconsequential when I see the extensive and extreme problems in the world."

Robert vowed to return the next summer with a team who would help those living in that strange, beautiful, and impoverished environment.

As the time approached to return to the Philippine mission, Robert recruited a team. This time, he wanted to bring Brenda with him, and he thought of asking his friend, Kevin Dixon, to join them.

Kevin was doing some work for Joe and knew of Joe's enthusiasm for mission work. When Robert told Kevin that he was looking for people to go with him to the mission in the Philippines, Kevin listened and readily agreed to go with him.

That summer of 1989, Kevin, Robert, and Brenda met others on the mission trip that they would never forget, like huge, happy-go-lucky Percy and Rudy who was to later become a bishop.

Another fellow missioner, Tony, went on to become the head of United Methodist Volunteers in Mission (UMVIM) and ultimately, a Methodist minister. But an ordinary Filipino carpenter made the most profound impression on them.

In his work with local missions, Robert learned from his father to leave tools with those he came to serve, so on this mission, Robert gave one of the local Filipino workers a nail pouch, tape measure, handsaw, and hammer.

The man returned to the mission site the next day and invited Robert and Kevin to lunch. They walked a mile and a half down a dirt road in the midst of palm and pineapple trees until they reached a thatch hut with a dirt floor, swept clean.

While they waited, the man chased, caught, killed, and cooked a scrawny chicken. He gave the chicken and all the food they had prepared to Robert and Kevin.

He and his wife and children and his parents stood quietly by and watched them eat. Robert, feeling surprised and awkward, hesitated. Robert started to urge the family to eat with them.

Kevin stopped him and quietly advised,

>"Don't insult them. Eat it, and enjoy it, and accept their gift. When you gave him those tools, you gave him a career. He can show up now and be a carpenter. You changed his life."

And those they came to serve changed Kevin's life, just as they had changed Robert's. After the first mission trip with Robert and Brenda, Kevin added his passion and enthusiasm to every team Bethany sent.

Kevin joined Joe, Jackie and Martha Jo Roumillat, Tim and Kathy McConnell, Casey Canonge, George Keifer, and a growing number of Bethany members who formed the Bethany Global mission team.

Over the next 22 years, with Joe's instigation, Bethany's mission team made many trips to an area in Jeremi, Haiti, returning to expand and renovate the clinic, and add an operating room.

They built an orphanage, a dental clinic, and a tuberculosis clinic as well as churches, workshops, and other buildings.

The trips to Haiti fed the fire that God set in Joe, and he devoted more and more of his time and resources to mission work.

He continued to serve near his home in South Carolina, and he frequently led the charge to respond to the needs of other states like North Carolina, West Virginia,

Kentucky, Mississippi, Georgia, Louisiana, and Alabama.

And he didn't hesitate to answer the call to go to other countries, including the Virgin Islands, Honduras, and Romania, and, after over four decades of separation, he was able to respond to needs in his home country of Lithuania.

Without setting foot there, he found a way to serve people suffering in West Africa during the 2014 Ebola outbreak. His next mission is to find a way to help the people of the Bahamas struggling to recover from the direct and devasting hit of Category 5 Hurricane Dorian in 2019.

Joe was the person who led the drive to raise the money to go on a mission trip, and if they were on a trip and some poor soul came to them with a need, Joe would be the first to get his wallet and peel out the bills to give to them.

The others called Joe the Pied Piper because he always had candy or change in his pocket, and he never learned that if he gave out one piece of candy, he'd have to give out 50.

This was not recommended behavior, and Joe's tendency to disregard the UVIM policy to stay within a pre-set budget and give through the proper channels often got him in trouble.

When Casey Canonge, a faithful member of the global mission team, was in charge of the team, as he often was, he tried to counsel Joe.

Casey patiently explained that Joe should follow the protocol to avoid misunderstandings or trouble, but Joe never listened, and Casey had a hard time keeping Joe from giving away candy and all of his money.

Everyone knew it was Joe who made the mission trips happen. He was the one who motivated the volunteers, and with his great sense of humor, he kept them laughing and in good spirits.

Joe loved to tease people, and they enjoyed teasing him back and picking on him a little, but Joe took it all with a laugh. Kevin got away with teasing Joe the most because he knew him so well from either working for him or working with him for so long.

Kevin kept the others laughing telling stories on Joe, and he could imitate Joe's accent perfectly, but it was clear that he loved Joe and admired his big heart. Joe loved Kevin for the same reason.

For a time, disasters at home and in nearby states demanded Joe's attention. In late September1989, the catastrophic category 5 Hurricane Hugo caused widespread damage in Joe's town and throughout the Carolinas.

South Carolina suffered the worst impact where 3,307 homes were destroyed, and 18,171 homes sustained major damage. Over 12,600 mobile homes and 18,000 multi–family houses were damaged or destroyed, and over 100,000 people were left homeless.

Joe volunteered to help with hurricane relief and immediately began in his own town of Summerville where he repaired and renovated Dr. Fredrick Yabuah's severely damaged home.

He was then sent to McClellanville and Awendaw where the devastation was even worse. In McClellanville, he rebuilt a parsonage to replace the one that had been wiped out during the storm.

Other churches were supposed to send volunteers to help, but Joe ended up doing all the work including the plumbing, heat, and air.

Then Robert and Jackie joined him to construct a home for the caretaker of the Sewee Retreat Center, a Methodist center that was reopening after recovering from Hugo.

They listened to the stories of people who had lost their homes and survived the hurricane by climbing into the rafters and clinging onto them as the water rose, certain that they were going to die.

After they finished the caretaker's home, Robert and Joe returned to rebuild other damaged homes. They were amazed that all of the houses in the area had water lines two feet from their rooftops, and they thanked God that more people didn't die.

A couple of years after Hugo, a Bethany member came to Joe and told him that the nearby Edisto Indian tribe was in dire need of a medical clinic. Joe funded it himself and organized and directed volunteers from church to help him build it.

In addition to building the clinic, Joe and the Bethany volunteers took on the repair of some of the people's homes that were still in disrepair after Hugo.

The team experienced a few setbacks like the one when the volunteer doctor fell through the roof of one house, cut his leg on the metal, and had to leave the site. And then another volunteer cut his finger.

Joe, (minus a few fingers himself), and eager to finish the work, took a quick look at the bleeding cut and said, "Don't whine on the job; bleed and whine on your own time."

However, despite incidents like these and the difficulties that came with accomplishing any mission, they were successful in building and establishing the much-needed clinic and in making the homes safe and solid again.

Joe continued to help those in need near home like the Edisto Indians. He kept the Charleston Orphanage house in good repair, and he renovated the Horizon House, a homeless shelter.

Joe also made many mission trips to North Carolina that had been hit by a series of powerful hurricanes and a damaging flood.

On one such trip, the team was asked to convert an old block building garage into a house for a family left homeless. It was just four walls and a roof.

Jack Roumillat and Joe tackled it, and in the first week, the bishop came out to see their progress. Joe estimated that it would take 10 days to finish it.

The Bishop thought Joe was joking, but when Jackie and Joe left 10 days later, everything was finished with bathrooms, cabinets, and everything else except the carpet.

The most difficult part of that mission trip was witnessing the ugliness of racism in the town. Because the home they built was for a black family, some of the white locals resented the help Joe and Jackie were giving them.

Joe went to a store, and a white man accosted him, demanding to know how long Joe was going to help those "niggers." They were disturbed by the racism, and they also had a hard time communicating with some of the people there.

At lunch one day, Jackie asked for a peanut butter and jelly sandwich. He asked for the peanut butter to be on one side and the jelly on the other.

The server prepared Jackie's sandwich and handed him a slice of bread covered with peanut butter on one side, and on the other side of the same slice of bread, he had covered it with jelly.

Despite the racism and the communication problems, they were glad they came, and they were happy with their job and with being able to help the family.

On another mission in North Carolina, the Bethany mission team helped rebuild an orphanage. For another one, they rebuilt a church that had been destroyed by a hurricane and condemned.

They had to fortify the church with beams and plywood on the inside walls. One young man, Daniel Rogers, was eager to go on the trip, and he brought other young men with him in a motorhome.

Joe assigned Daniel's crew a job he thought would take full week. Just seven hours later, Daniel and his team asked for more work. Later that day, they asked for another assignment and finished that, too.

Joe , whose standards were notoriously high, made a comment to the group, "That Daniel Rogers is a hard worker!" Daniel's solid reputation at Bethany was established, and it stands to this day.

Joe will never forget one particular mission trip to NC. He had to stay with other volunteers in an armory that had been closed for two years. It had only three rooms: a bathroom, a huge open bay, and a little office.

A team was already there when Joe's team arrived, and another team came soon afterward. Three teams stayed together in the building, including a youth group from Michigan.

Joe's group had their traditional devotions every morning. One morning, the youth group asked if they could join them, and they ended up working together that day.

Joe was impressed with how hard the youth worked. The areas under the houses were full of trash and mud, and the youth group went under the houses and "worked like dogs" to clean them out.

After work, Joe invited the youth to eat steaks with them. The youth wanted to pay Joe for cooking their meals, but Joe wouldn't take their money and invited them to continue joining them for devotions and supper.

One young man told Joe that he had given up a trip to Hawaii to come on the mission trip, and he was glad he did. Others told Joe that he treated them better than their own parents and gave him two big bouquets of flowers in appreciation.

The night before they left, the youth and Joe's team held a devotion and took communion together. As they blessed and passed the bread and cup around, they experienced a special bond that Joe never will forget.

For a long time afterwards, Joe received letters from those young people telling him how much they had enjoyed the mission trip and how much it had meant to them.

Then in 1997, Hurricane Marilyn ripped apart St. Thomas, Virgin Islands, so Joe was called again to take a team overseas to help them recover.

Nurse Roanna Payne had recently joined the church and joined the team on her first mission trip. Like the others, she became a dedicated missioner who went with the Bethany team as often as she could, eventually leading mission teams herself.

Not long after the trip to St. Thomas, a new preacher was assigned to Bethany. Neither Joe nor the new preacher, Bob Howell, will ever forget the first day they met.

It was a Monday morning, and Joe had been working all weekends and many nights for weeks trying to get the parsonage ready in time for the new preacher and his family.

Joe recalls that day:

"I had been doing all the work, and I had an appointment set up for a carpet man to come in at 8:00 am. He didn't show."

Meantime, Bob was having a rough start, too. Just getting the staff to cooperate with finding the time for a staff meeting had been an unexpected trial.

When he finally got them together for the first staff meeting that Monday morning, he asked if he could see the parsonage. He hadn't seen it yet, and he was eager to move his family into it. They told him, "They're still working on it."

Bob wanted to see it anyway, so he walked over and walked in through the front door. A little man came around the corner from the dining room into the living room and stood with his hands on his hips, looking him over with flashing eyes,

"Where the hell have you been?"

Bob leaned toward him with both hands on the back of the sofa that was between them and replied,

"I've been at the church."

Joe stared at the short, bald man.

232

"Are you the damn carpet man?"

"No. I'm not your carpet man; I'm your new pastor."

Joe paused, smiled, and then said wryly,

"Well at least I can look you in the eye!"

It didn't take long for Bob to observe Joe throwing himself into church and mission work. Not long before Christmas, Joe decided on a new project. Everything in the church was army green, and Joe said the church needed renovations and a new paint job.

Christmas season, of course, is one of the busiest times in the life of a church. To Bob's amazement and relief, Joe wound up the work just in time.

Then, on the Monday right after Christmas, Joe went to the trustees and said, "I'm going to renovate the gym now. It's a mess."

Roland, a trustee, objected, "You just can't do it now, Joe. People are coming to use the gym for the tournament." Their discussion began to get heated.

Bob, who had learned a lot about Joe by now, interrupted and said flatly, "It needs the work. Just let him do it."

Joe promised, "I'll have it ready by the 7th," and left the meeting. Joe started working on the gym the following day. Bob recounts,

> "Let me tell you. People came out and got to work with Joe. They tore out old, torn insulation and replaced it and repaired the ceilings.

> We did that whole gym with panels and white ceilings and lights where it had been a mess before. And it was ready for that tournament, just as Joe promised."

From the time Bob arrived, Joe constantly harangued him about going on a mission trip. Joe was getting ready to lead a team on a mission trip to Inez, Kentucky, one of the poorest sections of America any of them had ever seen. Bob agreed to go.

George Keifer flew the new preacher up to join the others on his first mission trip. The team of men took their own food and cooks and slept in the same room on bunk beds made out of 2 x 4's and 2 x 6's with mattresses laid on top of them.

The bunks weren't comfortable, and the nights were noisy with a cacophony of snores, including Bob's. Joe remembers it like this:

> "Bob was in Jackie's group, and Jackie worked his guys a little harder than I did.
>
> Bob was a white-collar guy, not used to this kind of work, and he would come in, eat supper, and just fall on his bed and die, dead to the world until the next morning.
>
> On the second day, I was lying in bed, and here comes Bob, moaning and taking off his shirt and falling in bed.
>
> I got up and asked, 'Are you okay?' and he says, 'Yeah. But that damn Jack is about to kill me.' "

Bob tells his own story about Joe:

> "I climbed into the rack about 9:30 and went sound asleep and had to get up at 4:00 in the morning to go to the bathroom.
>
> When I got back in bed, I saw a light, and wondered what in the world is that? I slipped around in the bed and turned my head to see what the light could be in the pitch-black middle of the rural night.
>
> And when I looked across the beds, there was Joe at 4:00 am reading his Bible by flashlight. Every morning he read his Bible before he began work.
>
> It's one of the most touching things I've ever seen: this fierce, independent man, humbled before God, reading his Bible there every morning."

Bob went on his first out-of-country mission trip to Haiti in 2001 with Joe, Kevin, and Jackie. They had worked there several times before, and this time, they were there to build a dental clinic.

Immediately Bob saw Joe's love for children on display. Bob recalls,

> "I've never known a man who cared more about children. If you go anywhere with him, you will see him give away the store. He goes with his suitcase full and gives it all away to everybody. That is his nature."

Joe made arrangements for Bob to preach in a church where people spoke Creole with an interpreter at his side. The interpreter, the wife of the preacher, had been educated in Ohio.

It took a little time to get their routine down, but then they fell into a smooth rhythm. He would speak, and she would interpret.

There were 500 people crowding in the church to hear the missionaries' preacher. Bob thought he was giving a short devotion, but the service lasted much longer than he expected, and he's still not exactly sure what the interpreter translated.

In 2002, the team went to West Virginia. Steven Knotts, grandson of Olin McCurry, Joe's night schoolteacher and principal, and Joel Roumillat, Jackie Roumillat's grandson, best friends, went with Joe and Jack on their first mission trip.

Joe asked them, "Boys, what do you want for lunch? You can order whatever you like." And they ordered and ate an entire 18-inch pizza. They told Joe, "This is awesome. Things just don't get better than this!"

They enjoyed the meals and worked all day on the roofs, singing as they worked. At night after supper, they went out exploring, and as soon as they got in, they went straight to the refrigerator to eat again.

They worked on the flooded home of a woman with three children who was living with a friend. Her husband was seeing another woman and didn't care about his family or the house.

To make matters worse, people had come earlier and told her that they had come to help. However, they needed money to stay in a nearby hotel while they did the work. She gave them $1800 for their hotel rooms and the materials for repair. They took her money and left.

She was suicidal when the Bethany team arrived, but Joe and his team got to work. The unfaithful husband came out to oversee the work a few times.

Joe shouted at him,

"Hey, Bubba. Come clean up this trash. Bubba, clean out that stinking, spoiled food from the refrigerator. Bubba, why don't you come put some effort into this?"

When they left the mission, the house was completely finished, repaired and put back in great shape. They even bought new furniture for it. The woman's spirits were lifted, and she stays in touch with Roanna Payne.

In 2003, they returned to Haiti to build a tuberculosis clinic, and then, in 2004, they went to a new place, Honduras, to build a medical clinic at an orphanage called "El Hogar De Amor" or "The Home of Love."

Bethany was blessed with excellent dentists who donated their time and skills on

the 2003 and 2004 mission trips, including
Tim McConnell, Joe Dorn, and Rob Beebe.

Together they took care of the dental
needs of many hundreds of people in Haiti
and Honduras.

After nine hours of work on his first
full day, Rob was overwhelmed by the
terrible needs of the men, women, and
children, and as other missioners had done
before, he went to Joe that evening and
broke down crying.

He put into words the call that
compelled Joe and the others to serve as
much as they could: "This is just a drop in the
ocean. We've got to do something for all of
these people."

Bob Howell also joined Joe and the
team on this eventful and unforgettable
mission. Bob thought Joe was looking for a
way to make him feel helpful, so Joe gave
him the assignment of getting some supplies
from the "Home Depot" of the area.

Little did Bob realize that Joe was
expressing a great deal of faith in his ability
to accomplish a difficult mission. He put Bob
in a truck and sent him 20 miles away on

twisting and rutted mountain roads where people drove like every man for himself.

After hours of treacherous driving, Bob made it to the store and got what supplies he could find. On the way back, Bob came up to crossroad and saw a figure standing in the road outfitted in camo, boots, and a helmet, and carrying a gun.

He motioned for Bob to stop. Bob slowed down, rolled to a stop, and idled his engine. The armed man marched up to Bob's window and spoke a command in Spanish.

Bob didn't understand the command, nor did he know enough Spanish to muster a satisfactory reply. The guerilla aimed his rifle at him and looked him in the eye. Finally, he asked, "Gringo?" Bob said, "Si!" and he unshouldered his rifle and waved Bob on.

An American missionary had lived at El Hogar De Amor for such a long time that his Spanish was better than his English.

One evening the missionary took Bob and Joe to another village up a mountain that had never seen pavement. They got in a four-wheeler Jeep and drove on a washed out clay road, filled with gullies down its middle until they were deep in the jungle.

They arrived at a village called Agua Caliente and were ushered into a concrete block building with a tin roof where a worship service was about to begin.

It was an open building with no windows, and 150 adults and 50-75 children crowded in the space to worship there together.

As Joe and Bob looked around the congregation and the surrounding village, it was clear that their situation was desperate. They wore the barest of clothing, and the missionary explained that they had very little food. A potato was cause for celebration.

Joe and Bob watched the service and joined in the worship. Then they saw a mother put her offering in the plate. She did not have enough food to feed her daughter, but she trusted in the Lord to provide.

Joe was touched by the simple trust of the mother and began to cry. He knew what it was like to not know where the next meal would come from.

As Bob reflected on his life spent in middle class comfort, he, too, was moved to tears, struck by the depth of her faith.

In 2007, tragedy struck the Bethany Global mission team when their beloved friend and brother, Kevin Dixon, suffered a stroke and died at the age of 56. All of Bethany mourned him.

The next mission trip was to Mississippi after another category 5 Hurricane, Katrina. Joe gave Michael Knotts the details and asked him to share them with his Sunday School class which happened to be Kevin's class.

Michael keenly felt the loss of Kevin, and Michael's son, Steven, had been encouraging him to go on a mission trip ever since his own experience with "Mr. Joe."

So, as he promoted the mission to the class, Michael made a decision to join the Global Mission team and go on his first mission trip in Kevin's honor.

Michael rode down to Mississippi with other missioners, including Robert's brother, Paul, who had become a regular and experienced mission worker, and Gillis McAllister.

Mississippi was still struggling to recover two years after the storm. Many coastal towns had been obliterated, and all of Mississippi was declared a disaster area.

Over a million people were affected and most had not yet recovered. The home assigned to the Bethany team was one of thousands of homes still in need of repair.

Michael was an English teacher who had little experience with anything to do with construction and repair, so Joe assigned Michael the basic task of glazing windows in the back of the house while he was repairing windows in the front of the house.

Michael, lacking confidence, came to the front to tell Joe that he had finished the job and asked him to come check it out. Without even looking up, Joe stayed on the ladder and said, "Damn good job, Michael, damn good job."

Michael learned that the first lesson mission volunteers are taught is that safety is always job one. But he also learned that even the most experienced people can have accidents.

Paul was using the nail gun when a nail fired all the way through a flimsy piece of wood and struck Gillis in the middle of his nose. Gillis yelled out, and all work came to a sudden halt.

Horrified, Paul looked at the nail protruding out of Gillis's nose. To his relief, he saw that it had penetrated less than a quarter of an inch, just enough to keep the nail sticking straight out of his nose, but Gillis wasn't badly hurt.

He quipped, "Just go ahead and call me Robert one more time!"

The inescapable corruption in the Haitian government and even in the church led Joe to make the decision to end trips to Haiti. He took the team on its final trip there to finish the orphanage they had been building.

On a previous mission, Bethany had sent $7,000 ahead for the church to buy materials for the building they were going to work on. When Joe arrived with his team, the money was gone, and there were no materials.

Joe also learned that the orphanage the UMVIM was building in Haiti cost $250,000 while a similar one in the Dominican Republic only cost $25,000.

Joe and his team finished the orphanage, but in order to be good stewards of what the Lord provided, they decided that they needed to serve somewhere else.

Then Joe was diagnosed with Parkinson's disease, and he had to cut back on his mission trips. However, he couldn't resist the call to go to Romania in 2013.

There, the team worked on the Veritas Project and built a school, a home for battered women, and a youth center for gypsies.

In 2014, he couldn't stop thinking about people suffering from the Ebola outbreak. He was frustrated when his doctor and family said it would be a terrible idea for him to go to West Africa and disappointed when they insisted that he stay home.

But he came up with an alternative idea and talked about it relentlessly. He insisted that he and Robert should take his idea to the next meeting of the Global Mission team.

They went to the meeting, and Joe stood up. "We don't have to go there," he said. "We are going to put on a fundraising dinner here and send money to help them."

He planned and orchestrated a grand gala. They sold tickets and filled every seat. The men's group, dressed in black coat and tie, acted as waiters and served a delicious prime rib meal to the happy crowd.

Joe made the appeal, and the congregation of his friends dug into their wallets. A substantial sum of money was raised and sent where it could help the workers in West Africa the most.

That's how Joe always did things. He would get something in his mind, go after it, convince others to join him, and get it done.

Joe with Haitian children

Joe cooks dinner to raise money for the
Ebola Outbreak

Part Five:
A Crown of Beauty
for Ashes

250

Chapter 15

Restoration

"And we know that God causes all things to work together for good to those who love God, to those who are called according to His purpose." (Romans 8:28)

After Jouzas escaped with the Ruzvyciuses during the Russian invasion of 1944, his family waited anxiously to hear word of him. Magdelena prayed constantly and often fell to her knees crying.

Anele could see her outside the window of their home on her knees burying her face in her hands and sobbing for her poor little lost boy.

She blamed herself. Why did she send the little fellow out to work? Why hadn't she gone herself to bring him home from the Ruzvyciuses before the bombing started? If she had, he would be with her now.

She missed him desperately. Weeks passed, then months, and then years, and when there was no word of the Ruzvyciuses or of Jouzas, they had to accept that little Jouzas was dead.

Life in Lithuania for the survivors of the war was as hard as ever. The Russians had complete control of Lithuania, and they confiscated everything. Lithuanian citizens were forced to work for the occupying Russian government.

Vitas and Antonus were both drafted into the Russian army and were away in service for two years when they confiscated her land, but Magdelena and the other children were forced to leave their home and work for the Russians.

The typical worker's pay was 25 kopeks a day. A pound of sausage cost 375 kopeks. A family provider had to work half a month for a pound of sausage.

Anele got a job making 350 pairs of work gloves a month. She lost a finger, but that didn't stop her. She got permission to work from home, made quota in a few weeks, and supplemented their income with side jobs the rest of the month.

Anele married, and she and her husband worked extra hard in order to build a house. After they built their house, Anele invited Magdelena to make her home with them. Magdelena accepted the invitation and lived with Anele for the next 25 years.

Still Magdelena mourned for Jouzas. As in the years right after the war, Anele would notice Magdelena grow still, and she would watch her eyes take on a faraway look and her face grow shadowed in grief when something brought Jouzas to mind.

Often, Magdelena got up and walked out of the house. Thinking that no one saw her, she would fall to her knees and cry out her grief. Anele watched her with pity and her own grief for her lost brother.

Then one day, after years had passed, a Lithuanian family who had fled the Russian invasion and bombing of 1944 returned home. They poured out the story of the terrible years they had spent years in the German camps and as displaced persons.

They told their friends and family of their struggle to finally make their way back to Pajevonys. And they had news. They had spent part of the war in a German camp where they saw a boy they recognized from home.

It was Jouzas. They brought the news that he had survived the war, and as far as they knew, he was still alive.

It was a miracle! The family rejoiced. Magdelena sobbed with tears of joy and thanksgiving and whispered over and over, "He is alive. Thank you, God. You heard my prayers. You spared my Jouzas."

Yet, despite her gratitude, she was still burdened with remorse. She had carried the guilt of sending him away from home to work for so long that she couldn't forgive herself for the life he lived apart from them. They must find him and bring him home.

They immediately started looking for him. First, they obtained a Lithuanian newspaper that had been published in Chicago with a list of names of people looking for their families.

They poured over the list, and suddenly they saw it: "J. Stasiukaitis." Could it be Jouzas? Had they found him? They sent off inquiries. Finally, the answer came.

This "J. Stasiukaitis" had a different birth date and wasn't their Jouzas. They continued their search exhausting all available resources, contacting every group or government agency trying to reunite families torn apart by the war.

Anele learned that two ladies living in a nearby village could write in German. She went to them and pleaded for them to help her contact German agencies so that she could find Jouzas.

They agreed to help her, and they wrote Anele's letters for her in German and sent out many letters to different German organizations. One of the letters was to the German Red Cross.

Again, they found a "J. Stasiukaitis" that matched all the facts about Jouzas except the year of his birth. Anele begged the German Red Cross to contact this "J. Stasiukaitis" anyway.

She wanted to be certain this wasn't their Jouzas, and she didn't want to risk the possibility that the authorities or a confused little boy had made a mistake.

As time went on, their hope for finding Jouzas dwindled, but they persevered. No one had heard word from him or seen him for decades. If he were still alive, and if they could find him, he would be a grown man now in his forties.

One day, in the spring of 1979, Joe came home from work and, as usual, checked the mail before he came into the house. Among the bills, he had an envelope from overseas with a German stamp.

Curious, he tore open the envelope, and found a sheet of paper inside with a note written to Jouzas. It was signed, "Anele."

Joe sat down and stared at the letter in his hand. He couldn't believe it. He read it again and again. And finally, after 35 long, painful years since that dreadful day of separation in 1944, Joe held in his hand the evidence of a miracle.

Anele was alive, and so was Salome, and Jonas, and Terese, and Vitas, and Antonus, and Bernadas. All of his brothers and sisters were alive! And so was his dear mother who had never stopped praying for word from her son.

Joe marveled that his mother and all of his brothers and sisters had survived the bombings, land mines, and Russian occupation with its persecutions and "disappearances" of citizens.

Even Jonas had miraculously survived three years of hard labor at the Siberian labor camp. After Stalin died in 1953, Jonas had been able to make his way home.

Joe was elated. God had saved them. The family he thought had been lost to him all those years ago was restored to him.

Joe knew from the news that conditions for those under Russian rule were terrible, and he learned that in Lithuania, his family was struggling to survive.

He desperately searched for a way he could help them. He learned that a company in New Jersey was able to get packages into Lithuania for $65 a month.

Joe immediately put together a package of items he knew they could use and money that they could convert into rubles. He sent off the packages and smiled to think about how glad they would be to receive them.

They would know for a certainty that their brother was well and that he loved

258

them. He eagerly waited to hear back from them. He waited a long time.

When he finally heard from them, their letter was overflowing with love and joy, but there was no mention of the packages. Joe kept writing letters and continued sending money and packages.

Finally, he realized that they had never received his packages or his money. Joe looked for another way to send packages to them. Every year, he sent money and packages, filled with gifts he knew they could use, but not every package arrived.

Joe knew that he had to try, and every now and then, a package would get through to them. In twenty years, they received four of the packages Joe had lovingly sent to his family.

Joe longed to see his mother and family, but he couldn't get a visa to visit Lithuania, and they couldn't get a visa to leave Lithuania to visit him.

Year after year, Joe persevered in his efforts to get a visa so he could be reunited with his mother and brothers and sisters and meet their families. To his sorrow, his mother died before they had a chance to reunite.

Then on Friday, June 12, 1987, in West Berlin, President Ronald Reagan challenged General Secretary Gorbachev,

> "... if you seek peace, if you seek prosperity for the Soviet Union and Eastern Europe, if you seek liberalization, come here to this gate. Mr. Gorbachev, open this gate. Mr. Gorbachev...Mr. Gorbachev, tear down this wall!"

> Reagan went on to add, "Yes, across Europe, this wall will fall. For it cannot withstand faith; it cannot withstand truth. The wall cannot withstand freedom."

Reagan was right. The wall came down, and, in 1989, a decade after receiving the word of their miraculous survival and 45 years after little Jouzas had been torn from his family, Joe, now 55 and a successful American businessman, got his visa.

In July, Joe packed four suitcases full of gifts for each family member and boarded a plane to Frankfurt where he would catch a plane to fly to Moscow. From Moscow, he would fly into Vilnius, and from Vilnius he would go home to Pajevonys.

He couldn't sleep he was so excited, and on the long transatlantic flight, he tried to imagine the reunion and what each family member would look like.

When he landed, Joe walked through the lively, bustling Frankfurt airport until he found the waiting room for those flying to Moscow. Russian people filled the room, sitting silently.

Joe felt as though he had stepped from one world into another, from a world of color to a world of black and white, from the sounds of life, to silence.

When it was time to board the plane for Moscow, Joe stepped onto the ramp and walked past a silent and somber corridor of Russian Army soldiers along the ramp to get to his luggage.

He loaded all of his own luggage onto the plane, not trusting any of it to get loaded by the Russians. Others learned too late that they should have followed Joe's example when they landed, and their luggage was nowhere to be found with no way to get it.

He settled into his seat on the plane and tried to recall the Russian he had learned when he was a small boy. The hours crawled as he waited to land in Moscow.

Even in the Moscow airport, it was clear that life for Russian people was not like life in America or Germany. Gone were the shops and restaurants and newsstands and food carousels.

Joe could find nothing to buy, no food, no snacks, no water, no soft drinks, no coffee. Nothing was for sale here.

The customs line stretched out as far as Joe could see, and the Russian officials were opening up every single suitcase and package. Joe panicked, thinking about what he had in his luggage and packages, and prayed,

"Oh Lord, what am I going to do?"

An old lady standing nearby with a cart spoke to him in Russian,

"It will take you one ruble to get through the line."

Joe replied in the little Russian he remembered,

"I don't have a ruble."

She repeated, "You need one ruble."

Joe said, "I give you dollars for a ruble,"

and he waited to see if the old lady would take his offer and give him a ruble.

While he waited, he prayed again. Then Russian soldiers came over to him and motioned him to the side. "Do you have any rubles, any guns?" "Nyet," Joe replied. And they let him through.

When he made it outside, Russians surrounded him vying with each other to help him handle his luggage, but Joe was afraid they could take his bags.

He couldn't remember enough Russian to ask for help and directions, so he went back into the airport to look for someone who could speak English to help him.

He found an information center where a woman spoke English. She told Joe to take a cab or bus to get to his hotel. Joe was worried about taking a cab and terrified that he would get mugged. She directed him to a bus and had him wait for her.

He paid her $20 dollars to pay for the bus in rubles. He finally got to his hotel where they showed him to a tiny room with a bed—even short for him, but Joe was so weary from traveling and stress that he fell immediately to sleep.

The next morning, when Joe woke up, he had a problem. He was hungry, and he had to have rubles to buy breakfast. So he went to the bank to convert 500 dollars into 365 rubles.

When he got close to the bank, a man approached him and motioned him over into the shadows. He wrote on a piece of paper and handed it to Joe.

"Do you want rubles? "

Joe nodded.

The man wrote again, "How much?"

Joe asked, "How many rubles for one dollar?"

The man wrote back, "700 rubles for $100."

So Joe gave him $100 and got 700 rubles.

The bank and the government would have given Joe only 365 rubles for his $500. They knew their currency had very little value, and foreigners were easy targets for a dishonest exchange if you trusted the Russian bank or used another official government agency.

Joe got some breakfast and went back to the airport for his final trip to Vilnius. The taxi driver wanted Joe to pay $20, but Joe told the driver that he didn't have it, and anyway, wasn't it a crime to exchange money?

The cabbie walked away from him. Joe got another taxi to stop. He also wanted $20. Again, Joe said, "I don't have it," and again, the cabbie walked away.

After several more tries, Joe realized that he had to get to the airport to catch his flight to Vilnius to get home. So Joe said to the next cabbie, "I'll give you $10 and 200 rubles." He got his ride.

On the flight to Vilnius, Joe's anxiety rose. He thoughts kept going around over and over, "What in the world am I doing here? I don't know anyone. I don't belong here," and then he realized that the people around him were speaking Lithuanian.

Hearing his mother tongue, he felt less anxious, and his fellow Lithuanian travelers reassured him by saying, "Don't worry. Your family will be there." It all started coming back, the language, the familiarity. He was coming home.

Joe stepped down the ramp from the plane, and when he looked up, he saw a group of about 40 people waving, smiling, and calling out to him. They had looked over the passengers and guessed correctly that Joe was their long-lost brother Jouzas.

All of his family was at the Vilnius airport: four brothers and three sisters with their husbands and their wives and all their children, some of whom also had husbands and wives and children with them.

But he didn't recognize any of them. A little, nearly seventy-year-old man who barely came up to Joe's shoulder walked over to him and embraced him and said, "Welcome home, Jouzas; I'm Jonas!"

Joe burst out laughing in surprise. When Joe had last seen Jonas, Joe had to look up to him. In his memory, his brother was a big man, surely over six feet tall.

And Anele came and hugged him, all grown up and middle-aged, and now Terese, in her seventies, kissed him, and Salome, another senior citizen, embraced him, crying.

Antonus, little Bernadas, and Vitas, all middle-aged men, hugged him and slapped him on the back. Everyone was talking and laughing and crying and making introductions.

He could hardly take it in. It was unbelievable, like a dream, after all these years to be together again. After 45 years of living another life in another country, it was like being 16 again.

Anele told Jouzas that he must first go to the police station and register. The officials at the station took his passport and gave him a telephone number.

Joe was warned that he could not go anywhere except for that town, but Joe's brother-in-law who was a judge and a major in the Russian army took him aside and said, "Don't worry, Jouzas, just agree and register." So Joe registered.

Then they took him to his sister's house where they had everything prepared for a grand homecoming. Tables were laden with an indescribable feast, full of wonderful, special Lithuanian dishes, and the liquor and vodka flowed.

It was a celebration unlike any other. At the end of the party, after the tears and the laughter and the stories, it was Joe's chance to bring out the gifts he had brought from America--beautiful clothes and much-needed medicine.

Then he handed them $30,000. They could buy anything they needed, even a tractor for the farm.

Later, they took Joe to a store for foreigners where he could show them his passport and buy things only available to foreigners who had any currency other than Russian. He bought everything he could think of that they might want and need.

Like Joseph of the Bible, the Lord had provided for Jouzas, and his own personal cup of blessing was overflowing. He now took great delight in blessing the family he had loved and longed for through the years.

He thanked the Lord who had brought them together again and who after their mourning had given them "a crown of beauty for ashes, a joyous blessing instead of mourning, festive praise instead of despair...." (Isaiah 61:3).

Magdelena's Funeral 1979

Joe reunites with family in Lithuania

Annual Lithuanian Family Reunion

Joe and Robert in Lithuania

Joe at his home church, looking at gunfire
damage from WWII

Chapter 16

Legacy

"Do you see a man skilled in his work? He will stand in the presence of kings." (Proverbs 22:29)

In 1980, seven years before President Ronald Reagan delivered the speech that would change Joe's life, Joe was impressed with the presidential candidate's message and platform and decided to donate his support to Reagan's presidential run.

Because of his contribution, Joe was invited to a large rally in Columbia, South Carolina and to dinner afterwards to meet the Republican nominee.

Joe took Harold Lewis, his minister at that time, with him, and they listened with approval to Reagan's plans for the country.

Three years later, in October 1983, Joe was given another invitation, but this time he was invited to a special dinner in

Washington, DC to dine with the now *President* Reagan.

It was a grand affair. Admission to the dinner was $1000, and each attendee had to go through a painstaking security check. The ushers seated Joe less than 20 feet away from the President.

Reagan was addressing the gathering when, suddenly, in a flurry of activity, security personnel grabbed Reagan and quickly ushered him out of the hall. The United States had just invaded Grenada.

Although Joe was disappointed not to be able to shake the President's hand, he was given documents to take home that President Reagan had signed thanking Joe for his support.

The poor Lithuanian orphan and refugee never could have imagined that the hard road he had traveled would bring him to have dinner with the President of the United States of America.

Joe's generosity and hard work on behalf of others earned him respect and recognition from the members of his adopted town. He became a well-loved figure in Summerville, both at church and in the business community.

The story of his life and of his growing list of mission work frequently appeared in the local papers, and he started receiving awards in recognition of his contributions.

In 1988, the Summerville Sertoma Club gave Joe the Service-to-Mankind award in recognition of his many contributions in recent years.

They included serving on the board of directors of Meals on Wheels, sponsoring a dream trip to Disney World for a child suffering from muscular dystrophy, building the eye clinic in Haiti, organizing Thanksgiving baskets for the needy, and building the home for Dr. Elliott.

Four years later, he received the Joseph B. Bethea Award, a Methodist award established by the South Carolina Conference to recognize outstanding service.

A committee used a strict selection process and scrutinized the candidates' contributions to missions in South Carolina. They informed Bob Howell, Joe's minister, that Joe had been selected.

Bob worked with a team of conspirators to get Joe to the awards ceremony without letting him know the reason for the occasion.

Their first hurdle was to convince Joe to come to the annual conference. To get Joe to come, they enlisted the help of Sara by making her a delegate, and they made up a tale about how the spouses of the delegates were required to attend.

When the bishop announced Joe's name and called him to come forward to accept the award, Joe was clearly surprised. He was completely unaware that the ceremony had anything to do with him.

He never presumed that he would get an award. In his own eyes, he never did enough, and he certainly didn't think he had ever done enough to get an award. Everyone cried: Robert, Sara, Kathy, and Bob, but not Joe. As with everything, Joe took it in stride.

Joe deeply appreciated these awards, but his greatest joy came from knowing that the Lord had heard and answered the prayers of his heart.

The Lord gave Joe a new home and a new family after he had to leave his family behind in Lithuania. He had marvelously restored his brothers and sisters to him.

Not only that, He had even equipped and blessed him to be able to help them at a time when they desperately needed it.

In 1991, Joe was prosperous enough to be able to bring his sister Anele, his niece, Jane, and Jane's husband, Gintas, to America to visit him and meet Sarah and his children and stay in the fine, 5000 sq. ft. home he had built.

They were incredulous that someone like Joe who didn't work for the government could have such wealth! Joe showed them his business and took them to his church. He took them on a tour of D.C. and on a vacation in Disney World.

Their most memorable experience was the first time Joe took them to a United States store, a K-Mart. Such abundance they had never seen!

They questioned Joe, "How many of these stores has your government set up to show foreigners?" They were openly skeptical of his answer. This could not possibly be a "normal" store where ordinary Americans came to buy their daily needs.

They walked around the store for five hours in stunned amazement without purchasing anything. Joe experienced the abundance and freedoms given to Americans through their eyes.

He was more thankful than ever that the Lord, in His mysterious plan, had brought him here and given him the means to bless his family here and in Lithuania and to bless others at home and around the world.

However, Joe had trusted his most fervent prayer into the Lord's hands nearly twenty years earlier, and during all those years, the Lord had been at work in Paul's heart.

With the birth of his own son, Simon, Paul realized that he couldn't continue to live the way he had been--working in nightclubs and enjoying the party night life. He tried to get his life together and got rid of the drugs.

As Paul got older and endured difficult experiences, including a bad marriage that fell apart, he began to mature, and he gained a new appreciation for his father.

With his own increased responsibilities, Paul realized that the reason his father had worked all the time was to provide for his family.

As a father himself now, he began to understand that the reason his dad was so strict and insistent on holding the line was for his children's sake.

Paul accepted the job that Robert offered him when Robert started Lowcountry Case and Millwork, and now he worked with Robert and earned a steady income.

Joe breathed a sigh of relief and thanked God for the signs of positive change, and he trusted Him to bring Paul the rest of the way home. In 2003, He did just that.

Paul married Crystal, the Christian daughter of a minister, in 2003. Marriage to Crystal started to change Paul. Crystal, with her quiet and unwavering faith, was even able to get Paul to go with her to church where his father worshipped.

However, Paul still rejected the faith. Earlier, he had started his own business, and now, when he felt he needed success the most, it failed.

He had a new marriage with a beloved young wife, a nine-year old son to support, a house with a mortgage he couldn't make, and he was at a loss for what to do.

Then he heard the Lord saying, "Are you broken enough now that you'll get down on your knees?" Paul answered, "Yes, I am." And he got down on his knees. By the end of his prayer, Paul's conversion was complete.

Paul gives his father credit for making sure that he knew what he needed to do when the moment came. Even through all their fights, Paul says his father had planted the seeds of faith in his heart.

Paul had watched his father faithfully attend church and read and study the Bible every day. His father had taught him how to get down on his knees to pray. After Paul's conversion, he told Joe about it, and Joe's final prayer was answered.

They still had a few knock-down-drag-out fights, but a new bond of mutual understanding strengthened between them.

Like any father and son who work together, they might bicker at times, but they also regularly go to lunch together and play "who can get the bill faster." Somehow Joe always manages to get the bill.

When Paul speaks of Joe, Paul says,
> "He's a great man. I just hope to grow up to be a fraction of who he is and do a fraction of what he's done for other people.
>
> In the past, we only butted heads, but now I can't believe how much I'm like him. We share the same values. We even snort at the same things.
>
> I have enormous respect for him. You know, God has a sense of humor. I used to think Pop didn't understand me or know anything. Now my son thinks I'm as dumb as a box of hammers."

Paul adds thoughtfully,

> "Pop taught me to work—no matter what you do, it's going to involve work and a lot of it. He's taught me his faith.
>
> I finally get where he is, and where he's been, and what he's gotten on his whole journey. These are the cornerstones of life. Truthfully, you can't go wrong if you have faith...and if you're a hard worker."

In 2006, Joe was reminded of how much people cared for him and his family when Lowcountry Case and Millwork, Robert's business, had a terrible fire.

On a Thursday evening, chemicals kept in the facility spontaneously combusted. When Joe came in with Robert, Paul, and his son-in-law on Friday morning, a hundred people were waiting for them, ready to help in any way they could.

With the help of these friends, including Ken Willard who let them use his shop to do their work, Robert and his employees were able to make their deadlines.

Joe continued to work at Lowcountry Case and Millwork until he was 83. He came in at 7:30 every day four days a week until his last year when he started to come in at 8:00 or 9:00.

He stayed until he wasn't having fun, sometimes until noon, and sometimes until four. Usually his back or legs would send him home.

Joe called Jack from time to time to check on him.

"Jack, what are you doing?"

"Joe, why don't you quit working. Get Sara and go on a little trip."

Joe replied, "I'm just like you, Jack, what do you do if you're not working?"

What Joe did when he wasn't working was to go on mission trips, but when his avenues of service were no longer open to him, he just decided to find another way to keep serving Jesus. Ray Litts recommended that Joe become a Stephen Minister.

In 2015, Joe went through Stephen Ministry training so he could show the love of Jesus to those who needed someone to listen to them and care for them as they were going through difficult times.

Several of the ministers whom Joe served and befriended since joining Bethany United Methodist church in 1970 described how they feel about Joe.

Needham Williamson, the minister who first urged Joe to start a mission team, once said, "While small in stature, Joe Stasiukaitis is a giant in terms of his love for God, for people, and especially those less fortunate among us."

Bob Howell, his minister for 18 years, says, "Joe is one of the finest human beings I've ever known. He doesn't even understand this about himself...but he is an example of saved by grace."

Ray Litts, the associate pastor who named his son after Joe, once told him,

"Joe, you're my hero."

Joe answered, "You don't know all the bad things I've done,"

"I know who you are today, Joe, and you're my hero. You have become the man I want to be, tenacious, generous, hard-working, and a constant friend."

Ray added simply, "I love him."

Like Ray, Harold Lewis ended a long interview about Joe with these words, "I want Joe to know that I love him."

In the Old Testament, we can see that God was present with Joseph through all the events of his life, and we learn how God took his terrible circumstances and turned them into His good purposes.

In the Genesis story, Joseph's life was suddenly changed from one of love and security to one of slavery, betrayed by his own brothers. He was taken far away from his home and family into a foreign land.

He went through many ordeals, including unjust imprisonment. In the end, every event brought him to the position that God had ordained for him, a position through which God enabled him to save many others, including his own family.

Joseph of the Bible never doubted God's providence, and he trusted God to keep him in His perfect will. The Bible records Joseph's insight for us:

"You intended to harm me, but God intended it for good to accomplish what is now being done, the saving of many lives." (Genesis 50:20 NIV)

Like the story of the biblical Joseph, the story of our American Joseph teaches us that God can use our most painful times for good, too. The painful circumstances of Joe's life led him ultimately to the realization of how much God loves him.

In His amazing plan for the little Lithuanian war orphan refugee, the Lord led Joe to touch thousands of lives in various parts of the world during his fifty plus years of faithfully serving Him.

The Bethany Global mission team that Joe started in 1987 thrives thanks to him and his energetic devotion. The Bethany congregation continues to worship in the beautiful sanctuary he helped build.

Meals are delivered daily in Summerville to those who need them. Orphans have shelter; sick people have medical care; and people worship in churches he helped to build in other countries. And the list goes on and on.

Robert summed it up well: "I think of Dad whenever I think of the saying, 'Any fool can count the number of seeds in an apple, but only God knows the number of apples in a seed.' "

Joe's hope is for the message of his life to lead others to receive God's love and trust Him to make them new, give them purpose, and strengthen them for life's trials until He leads them home to Him.

On Honor Flight Trip to Washington,
DC, 2014

"The LORD your God is with you, he is mighty to save. He will take great delight in you, he will quiet you with his love, he will rejoice over you with singing." Zephaniah 3:17

Made in the USA
Lexington, KY
07 December 2019

58264474R00177